BUYING
AND SELLING
A BUSINESS

BUYING AND SELLING A BUSINESS

A STEP-BY-STEP GUIDE

Robert F. Klueger

JOHN WILEY & SONS
New York • Chichester • Brisbane • Toronto • Singapore

ISBN 0-471-60311-2 (cloth)
ISBN 0-471-60312-0 (pbk)

Printed in the United States of America

10 9 8 7 6 5 4 3

PREFACE

On July 13, 1978, Henry Ford II fired Lee Iacocca as president of the Ford Motor Company. Suddenly, without warning and without explanation, after thirty-two years of service to Ford, he was gone. As Iacocca relates in his autobiography, Iacocca had reason to believe that before he was fired his telephone had been tapped and that spies had rifled through his desk at night. After he was fired, associates who had been his personal friends for years were afraid to visit his home, or even be seen speaking to him. Had they been discovered socializing with him, *they* might have been fired. It didn't matter that Iacocca, who had ushered in the Ford Mustang, had been largely responsible for Ford's greatest success. As one commentator wrote after Iacocca had been axed, ''If it could happen to Iacocca, it could happen to anyone.''

Sound familiar? Of course it does. It happens every day, and it's happened to most of us. We've all been dependent on the whims and moods of others for our livelihoods. We define our success, pin our hopes, and chart our futures on the companies they own or manage, never knowing whether one day, the roulette wheel will land on 0 and everything will be lost. Even if the organization and its managers treat us with kindness, the very size of the organization has a tendency to rob us of our creativity and imagination. Organizations must be run just so. Often management prefers to run them exactly the way they've always been run. The employees are meant to fill boxes on organization charts, to fulfill job descriptions that have been filled by scores of people in the past and will be filled by many more successors in the future. Try to apply your imagination and drive and you become a boat rocker, a rate buster. Before you know it, you're applying your creativity to your resume. The firing of Lee Iacocca is, in one key respect, no different from what almost every secretary, janitor, salesman, or executive must suffer: There's a big difference between working in a company and owning one.

There's another good reason for owning a business: You can make more money. Unless you can hit forty home runs a year or succeed to the presidency of Ford, you've a far better chance at big money by meeting a payroll than being on one, factoring someone else's salary into your profits than having your salary factored into someone else's profits. And this is as it should be. As the owner of a business you incur the risk; it's your capital that could be lost. As the owner you can succeed spectacularly or you can go bankrupt. If you're free to go bankrupt, you should be free to get rich.

What's owning a business about? It's about freedom: the freedom to maximize your potential—to put your creativity, your imagination, and your drive directly to work—without filtering it through someone else's organization, some other owner's ideas. Owning a business carries as many stresses, heartaches, fears, and terrors as being an employee. But there's still a difference between being exploited by others and "exploiting" your own energies. Our culture is grounded on the concept of free will. But having been granted free will, too many of us, because of inertia, fear, or bad luck, forfeit our free will to others, at least on the job. This book is for those few in our society who are willing to take the risk involved in exercising free will. It's written to help you find the business that's right for you, strike a good bargain, and get rolling.

ROBERT F. KLUEGER

Denver, Colorado
January, 1988

ACKNOWLEDGMENT

I wish to gratefully acknowledge the assistance of certain individuals who provided wise counsel. Of the numerous individuals the author interviewed, I wish to give particular thanks to Mr. Robert H. Pickering, President, Robert H. Pickering & Associates, Ltd., Denver, who assisted me in the areas of business plans and valuation; Mr. Mark Doran, of Business Acquisition, Ltd., Denver, who provided me with an insider's view of business brokerage; and Ms. Carol B. Green, President and CEO, Franchise Services of America, Inc., Denver, who provided keen insights into numerous aspects of franchising.

I wish to acknowledge the efforts of Ms. Dolores M. Jaramillo, who mastered my penmanship and who typed, retyped, and typed again substantial portions of the manuscript.

R.F.K.

CONTENTS

BUYING
AND SELLING
A BUSINESS

Chapter 1

HOW TO CHOOSE THE BUSINESS THAT'S RIGHT FOR YOU

"WHICH TYPE OF BUSINESS AM I SUITED FOR?"

Anyone reading this book is either thinking of buying a particular business or trying to find one to buy.

If you've already found a business you're seriously thinking of buying, read this chapter anyway. What you read here may reinforce a sound decision or provide you with some food for thought regarding the wisdom of your choice. If you haven't decided on a particular business, what you read here may be the most important and helpful part of this book. Throughout the book you'll receive a wealth of helpful hints on analyzing, investigating, and negotiating the purchase of a business. Believe it or not, investigating the financial statements and operations of a complete stranger can be easier than digging deep down and analyzing *yourself*, to see what type of business you'll be comfortable running.

Your Personality and Life-Style

Tom Brown had been an electrical engineer with a large instruments manufacturer for over twenty years. In the earlier years of his career, he really loved his work. He could sit for hours at his desk designing and analyzing electrical circuits. He became very good at his work and rose steadily within his company. Every Friday afternoon he felt a little sad, knowing he'd have to wait until Monday to get back at those circuits. As often as possible he'd take work home with him. He submitted papers to engineering journals and even spoke at engineers' conventions. But after a number of years a certain amount of boredom set in. What was worse, as he rose in the company he dealt less with circuits and more with office politics, since he was reporting directly to the vice president for engineering. But what really soured him on his job was that it was a *job*. No matter how far he rose (and there was only so far he could go, since the company was family owned), he would always be on a salary. He saw that some of his neighbors who didn't have his abilities but who ran their own businesses made far more money than he, and they didn't have office politics to worry about.

One of Tom's neighbors, Fred Ostling, owned a string of stores that sold stereos, radio gear, and records. Tom told Fred about his dissatisfaction with his job. As luck would have it, Fred told Tom the manager of one of his stores was retiring and, rather than try to find another manager, he'd sell the store to Tom. The asking price seemed pretty stiff; the cash down payment alone was more than he had in his savings. But Tom looked (briefly) at the books of the store and saw it turned a hefty profit. He was so dissatisfied he decided to take a flier and buy the business. Tom figured his background as an electrical engineer would make him a natural candidate to succeed in the sale of radio kits, batteries, tubes, and headsets. He didn't know anything about records and tapes, but that seemed like the easy part of the business: the records and tapes just sat there waiting to be wrapped up and sold.

Fred agreed to pay the retiring manager, Gene Downing, two weeks' salary if Gene would stay around and break Tom in for two weeks after the sale. During that two-week period Tom learned all about the business of running a stereo store. As he suspected, it wasn't all that difficult. The suppliers delivered, you opened the shop, and you sold the radios and records. He did learn a few things, however, that were disturbing. He learned that if you wanted to make any real money, you had to stay open after dinner, when most of the teenagers go out record shopping. In fact, the lease with the landlord (the shop was located in a large mall) *required* that the shop remain open during mall hours. He also learned Gene Downing's wife had also worked in the store, handling the invoices and the records while Gene dealt with the customers. Tom's wife was a nurse; there was no chance she could help out in the store.

Nevertheless Tom forged ahead in the record business. After about a month, however, he realized that while sales were OK, *he wasn't*. For one thing, he hadn't realized that staying open until 10:00 p.m. five nights a week could be so draining. At least Gene Downing had been able to take breaks or one or two nights off a week, since his wife could cover for him. Tom was pretty good with the customers who asked about plugs and jacks. But every night some kid wearing a black leather jacket or sporting blue hair would ask when Van Halen's new album would be in, and Tom didn't know Van Halen from Van Johnson, and didn't care either. (That's when he remembered that Gene Downing, even though a man in his sixties, seemed to enjoy rock music.) Most of these kids seemed to just hang around looking, without buying anything.

The worst part about it, though, was how insanely *boring* it all was. Except when he was unloading and shelving equipment, which itself wasn't particularly challenging, all he ever seemed to do was stand there, waiting for someone to buy something. It was simple, all right, *too simple*. It got to the point where he said to himself, almost every day, "I went to college for this?" His lack of enthusiasm started to show. He soon learned if you don't "romance" these kids, they don't buy records. He'd overlooked the fact that *record* sales, not equipment sales, were the bulk of the business. If they don't buy records, you don't make money owning a record store.

After three months in business Tom had had it. The long hours and the incessant boredom were driving him crazy. Fortunately, Fred Ostling found a person willing to act as store manager, and Fred bought the business back, for only slightly less than he had sold it for.

Tom Brown's story is repeated every day. The very worst mistake you can make is going into a business that isn't suited to your abilities and life-style. Before you set out to buy any business, you must ascertain where your abilities lie, what your interests are, and what about being in business will turn you on or turn you off. In short, before you investigate any business, you should investigate yourself. From the general to the more specific, your inquiry should go like this:

1. *"Where Do My Skills Lie?"* Tom Brown liked to sit behind a desk figuring out electrical circuits; Gene Downing liked to deal with people. It may have come as a shock to Tom to learn that dealing with the public, every minute of every day, was not for him. An understanding of his basic likes and dislikes should have been the starting point, not the ultimate lesson he learned.

Certain businesses place a premium on certain traits that others do not. Retail sales requires an ability to deal with customers. The financial and money management skills a manufacturing business demands of an owner are fewer for a retail sales outlet. Conversely, manufacturing businesses often don't deal with the general public. A business engaged in manufacturing or distributing often will entail a set of selling skills different from those for a retail business. Some people are good at taking potential customers to lunch and giving them the "silver tongue" treatment; others can't. Some people are good at selling *themselves,* which is the essence of nonretail sales. Others who work well with the customers don't work well with other people, such as the employees. Certain businesses place a premium on the organizational and management skills that dealing with a large number of employees entails. Some people prefer to work alone. Tom Brown didn't know it, but he preferred to work by himself. He was lost in an environment that required him to deal with others constantly.

2. *"Where Do My Interests Lie?"* Tom Brown didn't mind dealing with customers looking to buy electronic jacks and plugs, because he was interested in electronic equipment. He wasn't interested in rock music and could never warm up to dealing with it or the customers who were. It's very difficult, perhaps impossible, to succeed at something you're not interested in and aren't naturally comfortable with.

I happen to be one of those people who has absolutely no eye for style or fashion. If my wife doesn't accompany me when I'm shopping for clothes, I'm lost. How would I do running a clothing store? I'd be a disaster, no matter what my managerial, sales, or financial skills might be. Without a natural feel for the products I'd be selling, I could never succeed. Without having developed any interest whatsoever in style and fashion thus far in life, there's little chance I could develop the interest even if I were in the business. My wife, however, might do fine in such a business, since she has a natural interest in design. She wouldn't, though, do as well running a sporting goods store, dealing on a constant basis with distributors and customers talking the language of catchers' mitts and squash racquets. As the owner of a clothing store, she could easily impart her knowledge (and enthusiasm) to her sales staff. She could train a sharp eye on wholesalers trying to pass off the previous season's goods or styles that won't sell. She'd know which window displays would work and which wouldn't. Most important, she'd be able to help her customers find what's right for them, making them comfortable with her expertise. She couldn't do any of that in any business, such as sporting goods, where she doesn't have a flair for the goods being sold. Go with what you know or what you like. You'll do better.

3. *"Is My Life-Style Suited to This Type of Business?"* Even if you've a natural feel for a certain type of business, it still may not be for you. The business may have to be run in a way that's simply unsuitable for you. Gene Downing could operate the stereo shop, a business that placed enormous demands on his time, because his wife could help out; Tom Brown couldn't. Certain businesses can be operated profitably *only* as mom and pop operations; if there's no mom or no pop, either revenues drop off because of reduced hours or profits go toward paying hired help. Certain businesses require considerable travel. If your personal life prevents you from traveling or you simply don't like it, these businesses may not be for you, no matter how easily you warm up to the products or services they deal in. Other businesses require heavy lifting or place other physical demands on their owners. If you're retired or disabled and can't do the lifting, the business may be suitable for

the seller but not for you. Don't plan on hiring someone to do the traveling, the lifting, or any other job that you can't or won't do. That the present owner performs those tasks for himself or herself may mean the difference between profits and no profits.

Every Business Has Its Own Personality!

We're getting into the realm of the analysis of a particular business, which we'll cover in depth in the next chapters, but this point is worth covering here: *Every business has a style and personality that it's adopted from its owners and that you'll adopt when you buy it.* If your personality and the business's personality don't match, you may have a big problem.

Here's an extreme example drawn from real life that proves the point. Western Distributors, Inc. is in the business of distributing coffee beans to restaurants and supermarkets. Phil, who started the business, buys coffee beans at wholesale, blends them, grinds them, and sells the blends. Mrs. King, who's always been something of a gourmet with a particular interest in exotic coffees, would like to buy Western Distributors. She believes she'd get along famously with the sellers of the imported beans and with the supermarket buyers. She even thinks she could expand the business to include a line of exotic teas and coffee-based liqueurs. However, there's one curious thing about the way Western Distributors is run. The only way Phil "motivates" his employees is by kicking them in the seat of their pants. What's worse, the employees seem to *like* being treated this way. The only way to get anything out of the office staff (receptionist, secretary, and bookkeeper) is to scream at them louder than they scream at Phil. In fact, the whole place seems to be at the edge of a scream all the time. Mrs. King even saw Phil physically throw a driver into the cab of a truck in order to get him rolling. In short, this is the way the employees are treated and *expect* to be treated.

How successful would Mrs. King be at running Western Distributors? She may do fine if she fires all Phil's employees and starts all over. But if she can't, or doesn't, she may have a real problem. Phil's able to motivate his employees in his own special way. His employees have come to expect that the business will be run in a certain manner and may not know how to respond if treated differently. Western Distributors has its own personality. If that personality doesn't mesh with the personality of its owner, the business may fail.

Every buyer must ascertain what the personality of the target business is. This is difficult to do, and impossible to do if one doesn't spend as much time as possible eyeballing the operations of the business. There're ways to do this, as we'll see later, but they're difficult, since sellers don't like people nosing around in their operations before the business is sold. But an assessment must be made. You wouldn't knowingly marry anyone whose personality is offensive to you. Buying a business is very much like getting married; you'll spend at least as much time with your business as you do with your spouse. Don't buy a business whose personality doesn't fit yours.

HOW TO FIND THE RIGHT BUSINESS

Let's assume you've got a pretty good fix on the type of business you're best suited for. How do you find this business? Unfortunately, most people select a business in the worst way: by hearing about one available business and buying it. Just as you probably wouldn't buy a house after looking at only one, you shouldn't buy the first business offered to you, no matter how attractive it looks. Scrutinize the real estate section of your local newspaper. You'll find listings for a number of businesses being offered for sale. Check out *all* those that look promising.

The best way to buy a business is to use a qualified *business broker,* whose business it is to marry buyers and sellers of businesses. The accent here is on *qualified.* Regrettably, most states don't have any licensing requirements for business brokers, and anyone, regardless of what he or she knows, can become one. In some states if the sale involves the transfer of real estate, the broker will be required to have a real estate broker's license. What this means, however, is that many real estate brokers do a little business brokerage as a sideline. If house sales are slow, they concentrate on businesses. Try to find a broker who concentrates exclusively on business brokerage.

Business brokers usually operate just like real estate brokers. The broker will have a series of listings gathered from numerous sellers, and it's the seller who pays the broker's commission. If you're interested in buying a type of business your broker doesn't have a listing for, he may be able to find such a business from another broker, and the two of them would divide the commission. Most brokers obtain exclusive listings from their sellers, which means no broker has a complete inventory of all the businesses available. This means there may be an advantage in visiting all the brokers in town, in order to get a fix on everything available. The better way is to find one really good broker and work exclusively with him. Since he'll be able to find out from the other brokers what's available, there's little to be gained in visiting every broker in town. Also, most good brokers will lose interest in you if they find you've been visiting the others. A good broker will work hard for you but only if the broker believes you've placed your trust exclusively in him.

The key to finding a good business is to find a good broker. Unfortunately, many aren't either knowledgeable or reputable. Many have little concern about how you'll do in the business just so long as they receive a commission. A good broker will try to find out as much as possible about you before showing you any business. Some brokers will do a lot of the things that need to be done to close the purchase of the business. Others will only bring the prospective buyer and seller together and wait for the commission. In this book you'll learn quite a bit about the legal, financial, and practical aspects of buying a business. After you've read it, test your broker. If he doesn't seem to know as much as you know about all the ins and outs of buying a business, find another broker.

Chapter **2**

EVALUATING THE TARGET (I): WHY IS THE SELLER SELLING?

Let's assume that the following events have already occurred. After doing an adequate amount of soul-searching, you've decided a business engaged in some form of construction is for you. You've always been a pretty good amateur carpenter and can speak the language of the building business. You also feel you have the managerial skill to handle a business that has a fair number of employees and outside sales people.

You've also found a business broker you have confidence in, and with that broker's help you've sharpened your thoughts about what you're looking for and what you can handle, psychologically and financially. Fortunately, your broker's inventory contains a number of businesses that appear to fit the profile. You've investigated these, but all save one turn out to be blind alleys. All but one either cost far too much or are too small. Some are losing money and don't appear to be good turnaround candidates. There's one, however, Houston Sash & Door, Inc. that seems like a distinct possibility. Houston Sash & Door manufactures windows, doors, and other specialty items for general building contractors. The company has been profitable and the asking price is at least in the ballpark. You've visited the plant on a couple of occasions and haven't noticed anything (at least yet) that might scare you off. Your broker informs you the company was founded ten years ago by its present and sole owner, Mr. Everett Houston, who for the past ten years has been the inspiration and driving force behind the business.

It's now time to start in on the serious analysis of the business, which may culminate in making a purchase offer at a given price and on stated terms. At this point there's one question you *must* know the answer to as quickly as possible, for it, as much as anything else, will determine whether you will buy and, if you do, how much and on what terms: *Why does the seller want to sell the business?* If you don't know the answer to this question with reasonable certainty, you don't know anything. Sometimes sellers are reluctant to tell prospective buyers the real reason they want to sell. More often the stated reason sounds suspicious. If you're not comfortable with the stated reason, keep digging; you've got to know.

The real reasons sellers sell businesses usually fall into three categories:

1. The seller isn't making enough money in the business.
2. The seller has a personal reason for selling.
3. The seller knows bad times are coming.

There's a fourth, but rare, reason a business may be offered for sale. The business may have been bought by a "business doctor," a person or company in the business of buying shaky or even bankrupt businesses, getting them on their feet, and selling them. This business may now be up for sale simply because it's the appropriate time to sell it. The first two reasons businesses are sold needn't give you great cause for concern; the third reason is the one you must be very careful about. Let's look at each one.

1. *The seller isn't making enough money in the business.* Few sellers admit to prospective buyers that the real reason they want to sell is that they're not making enough, even when the financial statements make that fact obvious. Most often, admitting you're not making enough is admitting to failure. When a seller tells a buyer that the reason he or she wants to sell is to concentrate more on a new business he or she is developing or because he or she has

grown tired of business in general, the real reason is there hasn't been enough profits to keep the owner motivated to stay.

The fact the seller hasn't done very well shouldn't necessarily turn you off. After all, many businesses are bought and sold that haven't made any money at all and that have *lost* considerable amounts. These businesses are often sold for no more than it takes to pay off the owner's debts, if that. In any event the fact the seller hasn't made enough money will result in either a lower purchase price or favorable terms or both. One person's difficulty usually is another person's opportunity. If the reason the business had low profits was the inability or lack of drive of the owners, you may be able to turn the place around fairly quickly. (In some cases this requires little more than a new coat of paint and a broom.) What you have to be careful about, however, are the results of ineptitude that can't be easily corrected. The seller's lack of savvy may have irreparably damaged the business's relations with suppliers and customers. We'll discuss at some length an analysis of the operations of the business in Chapter 3.

2. *The seller has a personal reason for selling.* Businesses are often put up for sale even if they're in the best of shape. For whatever reason the owner simply wants out. Mr. Houston, who is about to turn sixty-five, may have decided that he's made all the money he needs to make and wants to retire to the Costa del Sol. He'll close the business if he can't find a buyer, but it never hurts to pick up a little extra cash by selling it. Similarly, a business may be sold because the owner is too ill to run it. The owner may have died, and the widow or the estate of the seller is now offering the business for sale.

Another personal reason for offering the business for sale, one the seller may try to hide from you, is the *business divorce.* In this situation a business has been run by two or more partners (whether or not formally operated as a partnership), and the partners now can't abide the very sight of each other, much less work together. Neither partner will sell his or her interest to the other, or both realize that neither can run the business without the other. The only alternatives are to liquidate the business and divide the cash or to sell it. Business divorces are far more common than you might expect.

Regardless of the personal reason for selling, that the owner or owners need to sell represents an opportunity for the buyer. To a greater or lesser extent it will drive down the sales price or, more likely, require the seller to sell on terms favorable to the buyer. If the seller needs to sell, he or she may be more willing to *carry* the buyer, that is, to take a greater percentage of the sales price by means of the buyer's promissory note. Mr. Houston, who's planning to spend the rest of his days in Spain, may not be amenable to selling for anything but cash. If the buyer defaults on the promissory note, Mr. Houston is either back in the construction business or forgets about collecting on the note. Rather than accept a promissory note, he may accept a lower cash price. However, had Mr. Houston died, his widow might have agreed to being paid over an extended period of time, particularly if the alternative was liquidating the business. If the business divorce is really nasty, the partners may accept both a lower price and a payout over an extended period of time, just to get out now. The key is to find out exactly why the business is being sold, and to calculate from there.

3. *The seller knows bad times are coming.* This is the reason you really have to watch out for. Let's assume that the financial statements of Houston Sash & Door reveal that the business has experienced a steady increase in sales and profits for many years. Nothing in the financial statements gives you any cause for concern. But Mr. Houston knows something you don't. A competitor has just devised and patented a process that will enable it to manufacture a superior doorframe at half the cost and in a tenth of the time Houston Sash & Door produces doorframes. The competitor is now gearing up to produce its doorframes on a nationwide basis. Mr. Houston is simply getting out while the getting's good. Sound like an extreme example? There're almost daily instances where advances in technology, methods, or marketing wipe out existing businesses or products. How would you have liked to have bought a diaper service six months before the introduction of disposable diapers?

Even if there's nothing in the offing that will affect the competitiveness of a business's products or services, there may still be some event on the horizon, known to the seller, that will prevent or impede the profitable conduct of business. Let's assume that the majority of Houston's sales are to one customer, under a contract between the customer and Houston requiring the customer to buy all of its doors and windows from Houston. The contract doesn't come up for renewal for two years, but Mr. Houston knows it won't be renewed. The time for him to sell out is *now*. As we'll see when we discuss the purchase agreement, Mr. Houston should be required before he sells to disclose all those things he's learned that may have an effect on the continued profitability of the business, on pain of having breached the agreement and having to return the buyer's money. Nonetheless many sellers, operating on the take-the-money-and-run theory of business ethics, won't tell you the real reason they're selling, and many sellers will sign anything just to get paid.

How do you find out the real reason the business is being offered for sale? You can start out by asking. If you have any doubts about anything you hear, keep asking. Don't be afraid to be pointed and blunt, even at the risk of embarrassing the seller. It's better for the seller to be temporarily uncomfortable than for you to be permanently uncomfortable later.

Regardless of what the seller tells you, nothing the seller tells you, either in direct response to your inquiries or in the form of formal representations made to you in the purchase agreement, should take the place of a thorough evaluation of the seller's financial position, which we'll get to in Chapter 4, or your evaluation of the seller's business operations, which we'll get to next.

Chapter **3**

EVALUATING THE TARGET (II): ANALYZING THE SELLER'S OPERATIONS

Let's assume you're convinced Mr. Houston's desire to sell Houston Sash & Door to you is legitimate; that is, the reason he wants to sell is truly a result of his wish to retire, not because he's learned something that's going to make it impossible to stay in business. Now it's time to roll up your sleeves and get down to the dirty work of analyzing Houston's operations, which we'll cover in this chapter, and analyzing the financial statements—the numbers—which we'll cover in Chapter 4.

YOUR GOAL: LEARNING ALL THE FACTS

Most of us are brought up not to be too nosy. We develop an instinct to mind our own business and stay out of other people's affairs. This attitude can be deadly when you're thinking of buying a business. Everything concerning the target business's operations is your affair, because you'll have to live with it all should you buy the business. You should take the position that *absolutely nothing* about this business is going to surprise you after you buy. You must drive yourself to learn everything you possibly can before you buy. This means being very nosy. It means asking embarrassing questions and pressing for details if the answers don't satisfy you. Only after you've convinced yourself that there's nothing more you can learn should you even consider closing the sale.

The problem with this approach is that a seller will often be unwilling to bare his soul (and his books) to you before you've committed to buy. Even if a seller has nothing to hide, he or she may not want to divulge the business's operations, profits, or trade secrets unless there's some assurance that the end result from all this time, effort, and disclosure is a sale. Any savvy seller will realize that if the word leaks out the business is up for sale, it may affect the morale of employees, relations with suppliers, and even the collectibility of accounts receivable. The seller's reticence may be reinforced by a prior experience with a prospective buyer who spent a lot of time snooping around without buying, especially if that prospective buyer later bought a competing business or started a business that now is a competitor. You, on the other hand, shouldn't be willing to consider buying until after you've received all this information. It's a classic chicken-and-egg problem.

Is there a way out? Often there is. In Chapter 11 we'll review the *letter of intent,* which should be the first document your attorney prepares and which gets the ball rolling. The letter of intent spells out, in very general terms, the buyer's moral (i.e., legally nonbinding) obligation to buy and the seller's nonbinding obligation to sell. There's one provision in the letter of intent that can be made legally binding: the buyer's promise not to disclose to anyone anything the buyer learns in the course of the buyer's investigation.

As we'll see in this and the next chapter, there're plenty of areas of investigation you're not likely to have the expertise in. What you learn in this and the next chapter isn't designed to replace the roles your attorney and accountant should perform. Rather, it's designed to show you all the things your attorney and accountant *should do.*

THE FIRST INQUIRY: "WHAT DOES THIS BUSINESS DO?"

Sounds simple enough, doesn't it? After all, we said Houston Sash & Door, Inc. buys lumber and manufactures doors and windows, which it sells to general contractors. Many businesses, however, are engaged in two or more different, but similar, lines of work; they have more than one *profit center*. For example, Houston Sash & Door may also sell a small number of windows at retail. It may also sell some lumber directly out of its plant to the retail public. Are all these activities equally profitable? Are some lines of work not profitable at all? Not only may the books and records of the company not reveal the relative profitability of each line of business, but the present owner may not have the slightest idea where most of the profits come from and which business segment is responsible for the most costs. A business only marginally profitable to the present owner may become more profitable in the hands of the buyer when the buyer eliminates an unprofitable line. You should also determine *how long* the business has been engaged in each line of business. Even though the business itself may have been established years ago, the main source of profit may have been established only recently; its future still may be in doubt. In short, your first inquiry should lead to a thorough understanding of exactly where the revenues come from and where the expenses go.

The next step in your general investigation of what the business does is to take a hard look at the products or services the business produces or provides. This is where you should try to find out how competitive the products or services are in the marketplace. Is the seller competitive in terms of *price?* Is price competitiveness maintained at a loss of quality? Is there a natural demand for the seller's products or services, or are sales generated through ferocious marketing efforts? This is where you try to learn if the real reason the seller is selling is because the seller knows bad times are coming. The seller may know that, while fierce selling has generated a high level of sales and profits, repeat business is unlikely because there's no genuine acceptance of the seller's products or services. This will be especially true of a seller who has been in business only a short time or has experienced a sudden spurt in sales. It is very common for sellers to try to pump up sales artificially in the expectation of a sale of the business. If you smell something fishy, keep digging.

LEASES

A thorough examination of the seller's lease should be high on your list of priorities. The lease may contain some news (including news the seller isn't even aware of) that may be so bad as to prevent the business from being sold on any terms.

Let's assume Houston Sash & Door leases its plant and office space from a local real estate company. Mr. Houston tells you what the monthly rent is and it sounds favorable. The plant is located close to a major highway; consequently you'd like to stay in this location after you buy the business. You ask Mr. Houston how long the lease has to run, and he tells you it expires in three years. With three years left on the lease, you could buy the business and take your chances on what's going to happen when the lease expires. Either you'll be able to negotiate a new lease on favorable terms or you'll have to move. But what if the lease has only eight months (or eight weeks) to go? Whatever you do, don't take the seller's word for it that the landlord will agree to a new lease or extend the existing lease. Before you commit to buy, visit the landlord and make sure the landlord will sign a new lease. If you can, get the landlord to sign a new lease with you, which should take effect only if and when you close the sale.

Even if the existing lease has a long time to run, *the lease may not be assignable*. If the lease has a provision prohibiting an assignment of the lease or says the landlord's prior consent is required, you must check with the landlord to find out if the assignment is OK. Get the landlord to put the consent in writing. Your attorney should prepare a *waiver* of the nonassignment provision for the landlord to sign.

In some situations the seller won't even be a party to the lease. The lease may have been drawn up between the landlord and the owner of the business, rather than the business itself. In this case the seller technically won't be able to assign the lease to you, even if such an assignment is permitted. What's worse, the seller may be a *subtenant,* so that the consent of the primary tenant, as well as the landlord, may be required. In all cases your attorney must be satisfied a proper assignment of the lease can be made. If it can't be, you probably can't buy the business unless you're willing to move the business to another location and the seller is willing to make payments on the lease although no longer conducting any business there.

The assignability of the lease isn't the only topic you need to discuss with the landlord. If the seller is behind in the rent or has in some way damaged the premises, the landlord probably has the right under the terms of the lease to collect these sums from you should you take over the lease. Find out if the landlord has any outstanding claims against the seller. If not, your attorney should have the landlord sign an *estoppel certificate,* whereby the landlord agrees there are no claims pending against the seller on the lease.

You and your attorney should read the lease carefully. Mr. Houston may tell you his rent is $5,000 a month. When you read the lease, you find, sure enough, the rent is $5,000 a month. But keep reading! You may find farther down in the lease it allows for an increase in rent. The increase may be a specified dollar amount or an increase based on a percentage, such as the increase during the preceding year in the consumer price index (CPI). The lease may even provide for a *pass-through* of the tenant's share of the landlord's maintenance costs, taxes, and insurance. (If the lease is a *net* lease, you'll be liable at the start for all these expenses, whatever they are, with the landlord receiving a fixed amount.) You may even find the landlord has the option to forget about the fixed rent and instead collect from you a percentage of your *gross* sales— a *percentage lease.* Your seller may not have had sufficient sales to kick in the percentage rent clause. But if you're planning on having greater sales than your seller, a percentage lease will increase your rent. It'll also require you to turn over your records to the landlord for inspection, so the landlord can verify that you're turning over a proper amount of rent.

Most leases also have a blank where the tenant and the landlord fill in what the premises will be used for and prohibit the use of the premises for any other purpose. For example, the lease may state: "The premises shall be used for the purpose of selling shoes and other footwear apparel at retail and for no other purpose." If you're planning to add a line of jogging shorts and shirts, it may constitute a breach of the lease. Once again, you should check with the landlord to see whether a change in the *purpose* clause is permitted, and if it's OK, *get it in writing.*

The standard commercial lease is very long and has the world's smallest type. Reading it produces eyestrain and brain damage. But there's just no substitute for having you or your attorney read it thoroughly before you sign.

LOAN AGREEMENTS

Let's assume Houston Sash & Door borrowed $200,000 from a bank to purchase the machinery that mills the lumber into doors and windows. Most of the $200,000 hasn't been paid back. You can be sure that not only did Mr. Houston have to personally guarantee the payment of any debt his corporation incurred, but that the assets he bought from the proceeds of the loan were put up as security for the payment of the debt. It's much the same as when you buy a home: a mortgage is placed on the house, and if you don't make the payments the bank forecloses. It's likely however, that more than the machinery bought with the loan proceeds secures the debt. Banks like to get all sorts of security, to ensure they'll be paid. They may also have gotten the business's accounts receivable and any other hard assets that weren't placed as security for some other debt. Even such items as patents and contract rights can act as security.

How do you find out the extent to which the assets are tied up as security for debts? The first thing to do is have the seller provide you with a list of all the debts and the files of all the loan agreements. You and your attorney should then sift through them, finding out the status of all the loans and the assets that secure the debts. But what if the seller "forgets" to tell you about all the assets that are tied up? No problem. Before you buy, you should check with the secretary of state or county clerk in the county in which the seller's business is located. They will have a record of all the *UCC-1* filings against the business. Here's how this works: Whenever anyone loans money to another and takes back a security interest in any assets, the lender files a UCC-1 form with the appropriate agency, either the secretary of state or county clerk. The UCC-1 form describes all the assets the lender has an interest in. The purpose of the UCC-1 is to give notice to anyone, such as you, who is interested in either buying the assets or lending more money to the borrower. A UCC-1 form says, in effect: "Hey, you! If you're thinking of lending to or buying from this person, just remember we have a priority interest in the assets! We get paid first!" The UCC-1 filing serves the same function that recording the title to real estate serves when real estate is sold or mortgaged. It gives notice to everyone else of a prior interest in the property.

You and your attorney must use the same care in examining the loan documents that you would use in examining the premises lease, and for the same reasons. The terms of a loan may effectively prevent a transfer of the assets. If this is so and the bank refuses to waive its rights, a sale may be impossible. Why would a lender try to prevent anyone from buying the asset and assuming the debt? Because the lender parted with its money only after it checked and was satisfied with the seller's credit rating. It may not want to deal with you. Checking with the lenders that have a security interest in the assets is one of the first things you should do. Even if the seller tells you getting the banker or the finance company to consent to the purchase is "no problem," don't take the seller's word for it; check it out.

Here's one thing you should *never* do: If the seller knows the lender won't consent to the transfer of the assets, the seller may suggest that the two of you simply don't let on that a transfer will take place. The seller will suggest you pay the monthly, quarterly, or annual payments to him or her, with the seller then rerouting the payments to the lender. You're playing with fire with a setup like this. If the lender ever learns you've attempted to circumvent the rights granted to the seller in the loan agreement, you may find the lender has the right to *accelerate* the loan, that is, call the whole loan. In this case you're stuck with an enormous debt due *right now*. It could kill your business.

We'll see in Chapter 6 that there are two ways to structure the purchase of a business conducted in corporate form: either buy the stock or buy the assets. If you buy the assets, you've no choice but to check to see that the assets are transferable. Even if you plan to buy the stock, the loan agreements still may prevent the sale. The lender may have obtained the stock of the corporation that owns the business as collateral for the debt. The seller may be prevented from selling the stock because the seller doesn't have it; the stock certificates may be lying in some banker's vault. Even if the seller still has physical possession of the stock, the seller may have agreed not to sell the stock until the debt is paid. Once again, make sure you read the loan documents to see if the business can be sold.

CONTRACTS

Your attorney should conduct the same review of all other contracts the business is a party to that he or she would do of the lease and the loan documents. If you plan on buying the assets of the business, as opposed to the owner's stock, each of these contracts will have to be assigned to you. For example, Houston Sash & Door may have entered into a contract with a designer to construct a window using the designer's plans, with Houston Sash & Door being obligated to pay the designer a royalty for each window sold. This contract may expire soon. If it does, the business may lose a valuable right if the contract can't be renewed. What's worse, the contract may not be assignable. Review all contracts carefully.

SUPPLIER AND CUSTOMER RELATIONS

Reviewing documents is easy compared with ferreting out all the information you need to know about a business's suppliers and customers. But when you think of it, there's nothing more pivotal to a business's success or failure than its dealings with its suppliers and customers.

Try to get a complete list of the seller's principal suppliers. You may find some startling things that will never show up in the business's financial statements. Is any one or a small group of suppliers responsible for most of the business's supplies? Have they been suppliers for a long time? How dependable are they? If one supplier drops off, can it be replaced? In our example, Houston Sash & Door may buy its lumber from only one source. It's very important to establish what Houston's relations are with that supplier. At some point it may be important to visit the supplier in order to find out if it will be willing to do business with you on the same terms it did with Mr. Houston.

Even if the seller has many suppliers and doesn't rely on any one of them, it's still important to learn about the seller's dealings with them. One source to go to is Dun & Bradstreet, which is a credit rating service for businesses. It should tell you about the seller's credit rating. Dig even deeper than this. Call some of the principal suppliers and ask on what terms they sell to the seller. If the seller's credit is good, you should have nothing to worry about. But if the suppliers will sell only on COD, it may be an opportunity for you. If nothing else, it represents a negotiating point that may lead to a reduced purchase price or better terms. If you can turn around the seller's bad credit position, the business may be more profitable in your hands than in the seller's.

The same holds true of customer relations. If the business is one that sells to the retail public, you can learn about the seller's dealings with its customers by visiting the store. But if the seller is a manufacturer or a distributor, you need to be careful. The starting point once again is to get a list of the principal customers and a breakdown of the percentage of sales made to each customer. You (or your accountant) should be able to verify the list by looking at the invoices sent to each customer and comparing them with the total sales figures in the financial statements.

Some businesses are dependent on one or two customers. For instance, certain auto parts manufacturers have only one or two customers: one or more of the "Big Three" auto manufacturers. Certain apparel manufacturers sell exclusively to Sears or Montgomery Ward. If, for whatever reason, these customers stop buying, the continued existence of the business could be jeopardized. I was once involved in a sale in which the seller had one principal customer. It turned out the customer was also owned by the seller! The seller had a guaranteed customer, but would the buyer have that customer after she bought the business? Our example, Houston Sash & Door, may sell the bulk of its products to one builder. The relationship with the builder may be of long standing and also be very personal; it may hinge on the weekly golf game Mr. Houston has with the builder's purchasing agent. In fact, the relationship may be so personal it may be *illegal;* it may hinge on a kickback Mr. Houston is willing to pay to one of the builder's employees but which you may not be willing to pay. In the film *Save the Tiger* Jack Lemmon portrays a dress manufacturer whose business is dependent on the whims of certain purchasing agents. To make a big sale to one of these buyers, he's required to provide the agent with the services of a prostitute every time the agent comes through on a buying trip. How would you like to find out something like that only after you bought the business? If your attorney is experienced in business matters, he or she will write a provision into the purchase agreement whereby the buyer represents to you there are no unusual, undisclosed business practices. This is still no substitute for your careful investigation.

PATENTS AND TRADEMARKS

I once had a client who bought a business without using an attorney. The business's trademark was very important to him, since that trademark gave the business's products a high level of exposure and acceptance in the public mind. This is the purpose of trademarks. Only after buying the business did he learn it had never owned the trademark! The individuals who had owned the business still owned the trademark in their own right and licensed its use to the business. He was stuck, and that's why he was in my office.

For starters, make sure the business itself owns all the valuable patents, trademarks, and copyrights. If one of the keys to the success of the business is a patent, which grants to the business the exclusive right to a certain process, don't take the seller's word for it that it owns the patent. Ask to see it.

By eyeballing the patent itself you'll be able to see if it's about to expire. If it is, the seller's business may soon face some stiff competition. Also, there's a big difference between being granted a patent and applying for one. I was once involved in a prospective sale that fell flat on its face when a patent attorney whom we brought in gave us his opinion that not only had the patent the seller had applied for not been granted, but that there was little chance it would be. Most lawyers (me included) are not adept at patent matters. If the existence of a patent (or a trademark) is a key to the business, call in a specialist.

PERSONNEL

If the business you're planning on buying doesn't have any employees or if you plan on firing everyone who now works in the business, you don't have any immediate personnel considerations. But if you'll be retaining some or all of your seller's employees, there're a number of things you should do. If you're planning on buying a successful business, it's a good assumption that one of the factors contributing to its success is a stable and motivated work force. Your goal should be a smooth transition, with the valuable employees staying with you and staying motivated.

Start out by having the seller draw an organizational chart for you. It may be the first time the seller actually has had to think about who gives orders to whom and who takes them; the process may be an education for the seller as well as yourself. Make sure the seller fills in the names of all the employees and their job titles.

Then have the seller describe to you, *in complete detail,* every employee's duties and who's responsible for the supervision of whom. If it's a small business, there may be only two levels of command: chiefs and indians. In a larger business there may be one or more intermediate layers of management. But even in a small business it's important you know what every employee is supposed to do. When word gets out that the business has been sold, it will cause a certain amount of discomfort for every employee, no matter how indispensable an employee is or thinks he or she is. Each employee will worry that the "turf" he's staked out is protected. Any special rights, privileged duties, or status symbols your seller has granted must be maintained or changed at your peril. Either way, you must know what they are. Examples abound. Your seller may have granted one employee the job of making the weekly run to the bank. It's a job that requires no special skill, but the fellow who does it considers it a badge of privilege. Certain administrative employees may have been granted certain privileges that plant employees don't enjoy (the most common being the escape from the time clock). Remove those little perquisites and you have a hostile staff on your hands.

Next, find out who answers to whom. It may not be obvious from a look at the organizational chart that one employee who has the same job title and duties as another employee is really that employee's boss! In fact, an employee with special skills or seniority may in reality be the boss of a number of employees. This is a relationship you may or may not want to change, but it helps to know it exists.

You may find that not everyone who works in the business is on the payroll. Mr. Houston's two sons may help out on Saturdays stacking lumber; Mrs. Houston may work in the office. They're not likely to work for you after you buy the business unless you pay them. To the extent you'll have to hire and pay people to perform tasks now done for nothing, your operating expenses will be that much higher and your profits that much lower. Remember when computing the increased payroll costs to include the increased social security taxes and fringe benefits you'll have to pay.

You may also find some relatives who *are* on the payroll. Their employment may be a form of private charity. If Uncle Joe's "position" and salary can be eliminated with no loss to the business's operations, the business will become that much more profitable when Uncle Joe is shown the door.

After you've learned who everybody is, what they do, and to whom they report, find out what each employee earns in the way of salary and fringe benefits. Don't forget that come Christmas you'll probably have to grant bonuses if your seller has an established policy of granting them. Even more important, get a complete picture of the seller's policy (if any) on raises. If the seller has granted across-the-board or individual raises on a regular basis, find out when the next round of raises is due. Learning this will not only help smooth the transition but will enable you to estimate your operating costs for the coming year. If the work force has been stable, find out what the percentage increase in salary has been over the past few years. Most important, if any employee has been promised a raise, get the details. If you don't live up to this promise, you'll have a very dissatisfied employee on your hands. Fringe benefits don't always show up in paychecks; the Christmas party, the annual picnic, the birthday gift, as well as the company's policy regarding sick leave, vacation, and overtime, may be just as important in maintaining employee morale. Don't jeopardize it.

If you're lucky, the seller may have already drawn up a personnel manual or company policy manual you can read. Find out how much of it is good guidance and how much is out of date.

Find out if any employees are planning on leaving. Lower-level employees who are planning to quit may not trouble you; the departure of a key employee or employees may harm the business. It's possible a key employee (a manager, engineer, etc.) has a written employment agreement. Read it! You may find some very startling information. For example, you may find the key employee has a *stock option,* granting him or her the right to receive a certain percentage of the company's stock if he or she stays on for a specified period of time. If this is the case, you're going to wind up with a minority shareholder—a *co-owner!*—on your hands. On rare occasions key employees have been successful in getting provisions into their employment agreements that give them the right to *veto* any proposed sale of the business. At the very least the existence of a written employment agreement will mean you can't fire the employee, should you want to, until the agreement expires or be liable for a hefty severance award if you do.

Closely related to the problem of employment agreements is the lurking trap of *deferred compensation agreements*. Here's how this works: Let's say that years ago Mr. Houston had a partner, Mr. White, who has since moved to Florida. Instead of taking a large salary, which would have pushed him into a higher tax bracket, Mr. White signed an agreement with Houston Sash & Door that obligates the company to pay him a certain amount every year as deferred compensation. If you buy Houston Sash & Door, you'll have to pay not only Mr. Houston but Mr. White, whom you've never met and aren't particularly interested in meeting.

And then there's the issue of labor unions. If all or some of the seller's employees are members of a union that has succeeded in signing a collective bargaining agreement for its members, the agreement will be right there in black and white for you to read. But even if none of the employees are union members, don't stop asking questions. Just because none of the employees are members of a union doesn't mean a union hasn't tried, or is now trying, to unionize the work force. Its efforts may have gone so far as an election to certify the union. What's worse, the seller may have committed an *unfair labor practice* in defeating the union. If this is the case, you may get stuck with a back pay award to a disgruntled employee.

How do you guard against employment agreements, deferred compensation agreements, and labor troubles jumping out of the woodwork after you buy the business? You've probably guessed the answer by now. The purchase agreement your lawyer prepares should require the seller to spell out all these lurking problems. But once again, it's no substitute for your careful investigation.

PLANT AND EQUIPMENT

Your seller may have the best of relations with suppliers and customers and the world's most dedicated work force, but it's not going to matter if your plant can't turn out the products your customers want to buy.

The first and most obvious inquiry relates to the age of the equipment. It may be going along fine now, but if the bulk of the equipment will have to be replaced in a year or two, a cash flow problem may arise. Most sellers who anticipate they're going to sell the business tend to neglect maintenance and ignore needed capital expenditures; it makes the books look better. As for major pieces of equipment, such as the milling machines at Houston Sash & Door, find out how old the equipment is. Then write down the names of the manufacturers and the model and serial numbers of each piece of equipment and call the manufacturers. They will have a record of when each model was built and sold. (After all, your seller didn't necessarily buy *new* equipment.) Ask them about the normal life span of each piece of equipment. If you're calling about machinery engaged in production, ask about the capacity of each item. The seller may have a lower level of sales than you think you can achieve by some creative marketing. But you won't be able to sell more than the machines can produce. You should also ask if the manufacturer has produced a newer line of better and faster machines; your competitors may already own these machines. Here's what you don't want to hear from a manufacturer: "The Model 150 milling machine? Heck, we haven't sold one of those in over twenty years. We didn't even know any were still being used. You're lucky it's still running because there aren't parts available for it anymore!" If you find yourself dealing with some really ancient equipment, you may even have a potential problem with the Occupational Safety and Health Administration (OSHA), a federal agency charged with patrolling compliance with industry safety and health codes. Just to be on the safe side, you might have your attorney check with OSHA to determine that using the equipment doesn't violate some federal safety or health standard. It should go without saying that if your seller has already been visited by an OSHA inspector, you should have all the details regarding that inspection.

Let's reiterate something we discussed a while back regarding loan agreements. Just because your seller owns these assets doesn't mean he or she can sell them. The assets may serve as collateral for a bank loan. The same holds true if the equipment has been leased. The equipment lease may not be assignable.

LITIGATION

Interested in buying a lawsuit? Probably not. Your attorney will have no problem smoking out any pending litigation when he or she gets around to working on the purchase agreement with the seller's attorney. Nonetheless, you should inquire early on about suits by or against the seller. As we'll see later, the existence of suits may have a bearing on whether you buy the owner's stock or the business's assets. If a pending lawsuit sounds so onerous that it may kill the sale, you're best off learning of it sooner rather than later.

If you're still eager to buy after reviewing the seller's operations, it's time to fine tune the analysis by examining the seller's books, which we cover next.

Chapter 4

EVALUATING THE TARGET (III): ANALYZING THE FINANCIAL STATEMENTS

The heart and soul of any business can be found in its financial statements: the *balance sheet* and the *income statement,* which is also referred to as the *statement of profit and loss,* (the P and L) or the *statement of operations.* Nobody would be so foolish as to buy a business without examining its financial statements (the books) before buying. The trick is to understand what you're looking at. Scan the balance sheet and income statement of Houston Sash & Door, Inc. (pages 32–33) for a few moments to get a feel for them; we'll cover most of the entries in depth later.

Nothing we say in this chapter is designed to replace the critical role that your accountant should play in your evaluation of the target business. You'll see why shortly.

HOW RELIABLE ARE THE TARGET'S FINANCIALS?

The first thing that should strike you about Houston Sash & Door's balance sheet and income statement is that both are prominently labelled "Unaudited." What does this mean? It doesn't have anything to do with whether the IRS or anyone else from the government has examined the books. Financial statements are either audited or unaudited depending on the amount of checking and investigating the business's own accountant performs before

HOUSTON SASH & DOOR, INC.
Balance Sheet
Unaudited

	December 31, 1985	December 31, 1984
Assets		
Current Assets		
Cash	$270,937	$104,268
Accounts Receivable (net of reserve)	230,962	139,917
Notes Receivable	60,142	70,812
Note Receivable—Officer	25,000	25,000
Inventory	203,841	205,778
Prepaid Expenses	2,500	3,500
Total Current Assets	$793,382	$549,275
Plant and Equipment		
Equipment, Furniture, and Fixtures	$ 60,868	$ 41,518
Less: Accumulated Depreciation	(31,592)	(22,227)
Total Plant and Equipment	$ 29,276	$ 19,291
Total Assets	$822,658	$568,566
Liabilities		
Current Liabilities		
Accounts Payable	$ 65,703	$146,713
Taxes Payable	2,040	2,335
Notes Payable	18,500	8,500
Total Current Liabilities	$ 86,243	$157,548
Long-Term Debt (at 13.0%)	$ 45,000	—
Total Liabilities	$131,243	$157,548
Net Worth		
Paid-in Capital	$ 4,000	$ 4,000
Retained Earnings	687,415	407,018
Total Net Worth	$691,415	$411,018
Total Liabilities and Net Worth	$822,658	$549,275

releasing them. There're degrees of care that go into unaudited statements. The big difference, however, lies between financial statements that have been audited and those that have not. If you're planning on buying a *closely held* business, that is, a business whose shares are not traded on a stock exchange, you'll most likely be receiving unaudited financials. Most closely held businesses are

HOUSTON SASH & DOOR, INC.
Income Statement
Unaudited

	December 31, 1985	December 31, 1984
Sales Revenue	$1,881,117	$1,832,286
Less: Cost of Goods Sold	961,330	952,557
Gross Profit	$ 919,787	$ 879,729
Operating Expenses		
Salary—Officer	$ 100,000	$ 100,000
Salary—Other	168,702	137,461
Bonuses	1,842	1,500
Taxes, Payroll	17,188	15,390
Advertising	8,920	8,550
Travel and Entertainment	51,220	58,110
Rent and Building	55,753	55,753
Utilities	27,139	26,333
Insurance, General	11,100	11,100
Telephone	10,958	8,752
Office Supplies	31,943	28,466
Professional Services	58,300	980
Miscellaneous	320	39
Total	$ 543,385	$ 452,434
Other Expenses		
Depreciation	$ 9,365	$ 10,891
Interest	5,020	1,122
Net Profit	$ 362,017	$ 415,282
Federal and State Income Taxes	$ 81,629	$ 2,770
Net Income	$ 280,397	$ 332,815

not required to have their books audited, and the owners of most businesses have no reason to undertake the considerable expense of auditing.

Nonetheless, there's all the difference in the world between audited and unaudited financial statements. Here's an example. Houston Sash & Door's balance sheet states that as of December 31, 1985, debtors (other than its own officers) owed the company $60,142 on various promissory notes. How did the accountant who prepared the entry know that to be true? Since the balance sheet was unaudited, the accountant probably didn't. The accountant might not have actually seen the promissory notes in question. Only if the financial statements were audited could we be relatively certain that as of December 31, 1985, these notes receivable represented true debts. In the course of an audit not only would the accountant have examined the promissory notes but would also have contacted the debtors to make sure the debts were real, hadn't already been paid, and weren't subject to some defense or offset that the debtors might claim.

Since Houston Sash & Door is a closely held business, there's nothing wrong or suspicious about its having unaudited financials. The next question cuts closer: *Who prepared them?*

There's no way of telling from a look at Houston Sash & Door's financial statements whether they were prepared by an independent accountant or by an employee of the business, perhaps even Mr. Houston himself! The lower level of comfort you should have for financials prepared in house is obvious. If the financials are prepared by someone on the outside, nobody's job is dependent on making them come out the way the owner wants them to. In those cases where the financials are prepared by an independent accountant, he or she will prepare them with a *report letter* outlining whether the statement is audited or unaudited. If there's no report letter, you may well be dealing with financials prepared in house. There's little chance you'll be able to require the owner of a closely held business to have an audit conducted on the books before you buy. But if the books have been prepared in house, and it looks as if you're serious about buying the business, you may be successful in requiring that up-to-date financial statements be prepared by an independent accountant as a condition of your closing the sale. If the seller is amenable and time permits, you yourself should select the accountant who will do the work (presumably your accountant, who'll be preparing the financials regularly after you buy). Who pays the accountant is a matter of negotiation between you and the seller.

Another factor that should have a bearing on your comfort level is whether or not the financials were prepared by a *certified* public accountant (CPA). Most people don't know the difference between an accountant who's certified and one who isn't. There's all the difference in the world. To become a CPA, a person must not only have a college degree but also pass an extremely tough state test. In most states the test lasts a couple of days, and most CPAs don't pass all parts of the test on the first try. When they pass all parts, accountants must obtain a license from the state board of accountancy. Many states require their CPAs to keep going back to school to keep their licenses. If the person preparing the financials hasn't passed the test, you can't be sure what you're dealing with. There're many fine uncertified "public accountants" and a few CPAs who aren't too swift. Nonetheless, if you're dealing with a set of financials not prepared by a CPA, independent or in house, it should lower your comfort level.

Let's assume that Houston Sash & Door's financial statements were indeed prepared by an independent CPA. Your accountant should look into a number of things before beginning to focus in on the numbers. The balance sheet and income statement on pages 32 and 33 are *combined,* showing a comparison of the business's net worth (on the balance sheet) and net income (on the income statement) for the years ending on December 31, 1984 and 1985. Comparative data are helpful but only if the methods of accounting employed in each year have been consistent. If the methods have changed (and to change accounting methods midstream is permitted) each financial statement should disclose this fact in a *footnote* which should appear at the end of the financial statement. The footnote should explain the switch in methods and, in some circumstances, the changes to income or net worth it produced.

There are some other basic questions you and your accountant will want to have answered.

1. *How Timely Are the Financial Statements?* Houston Sash & Door's financial statements go up to December 31, 1985, the date of its most recent fiscal year-end. That may be fine if you're reviewing them on January 31, 1986, but not if you're looking at them on November 30, 1986. Too much may have happened in the interim to give you an accurate reading of the business. If you're looking at these financials on January 2, 1987, an entire

year has passed. Presumably Houston's accountant is now working on the financial statement for the period ending December 31, 1986. Don't let yourself be steamrolled into a sale before you can see the up-to-date books. There may be a set of "interim" books for the fiscal quarter ending September 30, 1986; there may even be monthly income statements prepared by a bookkeeper. You and your accountant will have to decide how much value you wish to place on these interim statements and how much risk you want to take dealing with financial statements that are somewhat moldy.

2. *Single-Entry or Double-Entry Bookkeeping?* Financial statements are the result of single-entry or double-entry bookkeeping. Books kept on a double-entry system are always "in-balance," since there are two offsetting entries made for each and every transaction in which the business engages. Here's an example: Let's say Houston Sash & Door buys a machine and pays $5,000 in cash for it. On the company's books the Cash ledger will be decreased by $5,000 and the Machinery and Equipment ledger will be increased by the same $5,000. If the company buys the $5,000 machine for $1,000 in cash and signs a $4,000 promissory note, there will be *three* entries made: the Machinery and Equipment ledger will be increased by the same $5,000, but the Cash ledger will be decreased by only $1,000 while the Notes Payable account will be *increased* by $4,000. Everything must balance and this system produces financial statements that do. Double-entry bookkeeping doesn't prevent hanky-panky, as we'll see later, but does produce more reliable financial statements.

Single-entry bookkeeping doesn't necessarily mean that the business has been run sloppily or that someone has been cutting corners. Many businesses, particularly small service businesses, are routinely operated on the single-entry method, with the "method" being little more than the business's check register. A red flag should go up, however, when you're dealing with larger businesses, particularly ones that deal in inventory, that employ single-entry accounting.

3. *Do the Invoices Support the Accounts?* Your accountant should be able to confirm quickly whether the financial statements are reli-

able by going through the invoices. For example, Houston Sash & Door's December 31, 1985, balance sheet shows accounts receivable (net of the reserve for doubtful accounts, which we'll get to later) of $230,962. Like most nonretail businesses Houston Sash & Door sells most of its products on credit. By adding up the *invoices,* one should come up with a figure reasonably close to the figure on the balance sheet. If they don't, Accounts Receivable may be less of an asset than the balance sheet might lead you to believe.

What if there're no financial statements? It happens. Accountants will tell you about "shoe box" tax returns they prepare. These are tax returns that have to be constructed from checks, check stubs, receipts, and bills brought to them in shoe boxes and dumped on their desks. Often a business is losing so much money, or money is so tight, that it can't afford to hire an accountant to prepare the books. Does this mean you can't buy the business? Not necessarily. It does mean, however, you shouldn't buy the business *until* the financial statements are prepared.

THE BALANCE SHEET

What it is; What it isn't. Every balance sheet ever prepared for any business is *perfectly balanced!* This is not the result of accountants being mathematical wizards. Rather, it's because a balance sheet represents an *equation,* and the left side of an equation always equals the right side. The equation is:

$$\text{Assets} = \text{Liabilities} + \text{Net Worth}$$

or, stated differently:

$$\text{Assets} - \text{Liabilities} = \text{Net Worth}$$

Not only is every balance sheet an equation, it's an equation *as of a given moment* in time. Let's take a look at the balance sheet on page 32. It reveals the following:

$$\text{Assets (\$822,658)} = \text{Liabilities (\$131,243)}$$
$$+ \text{ Net Worth (\$691,415)}$$

What this means is that if we'd gone into Houston Sash & Door and taken a "snapshot" of all of its assets and liabilities at 11:59 p.m. on December 31, 1985, we'd have come up with $822,658 in assets and $131,243 in liabilities. The difference would have been what was left over ($691,415) for the owners. Because of this, Net Worth is frequently termed *Shareholders' Equity*. Had we taken our snapshot on December 30, 1985, or January 2, 1986, the assets, liabilities, and net worth might have been somewhat different, but the results of that snapshot would also have balanced.

How did we arrive at all the numbers for each of the entries (in accountant's lingo, the "accounts") on the balance sheet? By and large, balance sheets tell us only about the cost of assets when they were bought, *not what they're worth now!* Balance sheets tell us how much we were obligated to pay on the date of the balance sheet, not how much we think we're obligated to pay now. In other words, balance sheets tells us what things cost in the past, hence the terms *book accounting* and *historical accounting*. Does a balance sheet ever tell us the *real* net worth of a business? Never!

Take the Equipment, Furniture, and Fixtures account on Houston Sash & Door's balance sheet. It tells us Mr. Houston *paid* $60,868 as of December 31, 1985, for this group of assets. How much are they worth today? If you were to sell them today, would you get $60,868, or $6,868 or $600,868? There's no way of knowing. A balance sheet isn't supposed to tell you that. With this in mind, let's take a look at each account on the balance sheet, paying particular attention to its relevance to the purchase of a business.

Cash

Cash is the first item that usually appears under Current Assets, which are, generally speaking, the most *liquid* assets, that is, those assets most easily converted into cash. The Current Assets part of the balance sheet lists the assets in descending order of liquidity. Since there's nothing more easily converted into cash then cash itself, it's listed first. As a rule of thumb, accountants will place an asset in the Current Assets category if the asset is expected to be reduced to cash during the business's *operating cycle*. The operating cycle is the time it takes for cash to go through the business and come back as cash, as follows: starting with cash, to the purchase of raw materials, to the manufacture of finished goods, to the sale of the goods (i.e., the inventory), to the conversion of inventory to accounts receivable, and the conversion of accounts receivable back to cash when the accounts are paid. If the business doesn't have an operating cycle (e.g., a restaurant), an asset will be considered current if it can be expected to be reduced to cash within a year. The distinction between current assets and noncurrent *fixed* assets (real estate, long-term notes, etc.) is important; *a business pays its bills from its current assets.* On the day the Penn Central Railroad went into bankruptcy it had hundreds of millions of dollars in fixed assets but couldn't meet its payroll!

Cash is cash, right? Not exactly. All men may be created equal, but all cash isn't. The $270,937 in cash Houston Sash & Door had on hand on December 31, 1985, may not be freely available to it. It might have been borrowed, and the lender might have placed certain strings on its use. When you buy the business, you'll no doubt have to comply with the limitations. Also, accountants are given a fairly free rein to set up as few or as many accounts on the balance sheet as they choose. A different accountant may have broken out the Cash account into a number of accounts, which might have disclosed that part of the cash is in the form of certificates of deposit that don't mature for a few months.

As we'll see throughout this chapter, sellers often do certain things in their businesses to prettify their financial statements in the anticipation of a sale of the business. One of the things they try to do is increase the amount of cash. The easiest way to do this is by borrowing the money. This practice is somewhat daffy, since the debt will show up on the liabilities side of the balance sheet. When we look at Houston Sash & Door's balance sheet, we see there was a substantial increase in cash on hand from year-end 1984 to 1985. We also see an increase in Long-Term Debt (there wasn't any on December 31, 1984) and a $10,000 increase in Notes Payable. Has Mr. Houston been prettifying the books?

Accounts Receivable

On December 31, 1985, Houston Sash & Door was owed
$230,962 by its customers (net of reserve). The company gener-
ated these receivables by making sales on credit. As soon as a sale
was made, a receivable was entered in the company's Accounts
Receivable ledger. The $230,962 figure represents the total
amount of credit sales that hadn't yet been paid on December 31,
1985. Does this mean that within the coming year the business can
expect to receive exactly $230,962 from its customers? Not quite.
Every business has a certain percentage of accounts receivable
that go bad. The debtors go out of business, skip town, or go into
bankruptcy, and the receivable has to be written off. Not only does
every business have bad debts, but many businesses can predict
fairly accurately the percentage of receivables that will go bad.
That's what the *reserve for doubtful accounts* is for. It anticipates and
deducts all the accounts that experience has proven will turn out to
be uncollectible. The issue for a prospective buyer is whether the
allowance for doubtful accounts is adequate. If it isn't, the
Accounts Receivable account will be overstated, as will the resulting Total Net Worth of the business. How can you tell if an adequate allowance for bad debts had been made? Have your
accountant compare the amount reserved with the *actual* bad debts
for prior years.

Let's return to Houston Sash & Door's balance sheet. It shows
$230,962 in accounts receivable on December 31, 1985, up from
$139,917 on December 31, 1984, a 65% increase in one year!
How can we account for this? It may simply be that business was
great in 1985, resulting in an increase in accounts receivable. But
it may also be the result of Mr. Houston extending credit in 1985
to customers who wouldn't have received credit in 1984. He might
have done that to prettify the books in anticipation of the sale of
the business. By selling to customers to whom he wouldn't have in
the past, not only do the total current assets increase, the Sales
Revenue account on the income statement also increases. We'll
see shortly, when we discuss the *ratios* we pull from the financials,
that there's a sure-fire way to see if accounts receivable have been

artificially pumped up. For now, you should note that savvy lenders and brokers often request that an *aging report* accompany the balance sheet. The aging report is a breakdown of the accounts receivable by the length of time they've been outstanding. If a large percentage of Houston Sash & Door's $230,962 are less than thirty days overdue, there shouldn't be a problem. But if a large percentage of the receivables are more than ninety days overdue, there may be a real problem lurking. It may also mean Mr. Houston has become a little lax in collecting the receivables, knowing he's about to retire. Worst of all, the jump in receivables may be the result of Mr. Houston having shipped out some inferior products (again in order to prettify the books) and the buyers are refusing to pay. If this is the case, and the buyers who are balking are large customers or of long standing, you may really have a problem on your hands. After the sale uncollectible receivables aren't Mr. Houston's problem; they're yours.

A final word on accounts receivable: Every so often you'll find that the receivables that result from a business's credit sales aren't an asset of the business at all. This occurs when a business *factors* its accounts receivable; that is, a business sells its receivables to a *factor* for cash on a discounted basis. The debtors are then notified they are no longer obligated to pay the debt to the business; they're obligated to pay the factor. At first blush, it may seem that a business must be desperate if it sells its receivables at a discount just to get some immediate cash. Not necessarily. Factoring of accounts receivable is fairly common in certain businesses. Manufacturers would prefer the assured income stream that dealing with factors affords them, rather than dealing with scores of customers. If you're dealing with a business whose receivables have been factored, you should check the arrangement with the factor very carefully. Factors buy receivables in two ways: *without recourse,* or *with recourse.* If the factoring is without recourse, the factor suffers the loss if the receivable proves uncollectible. If the factoring is with recourse, the business still owes the factor if the factor can't collect; the factor is acting as little more than a bank lending money secured by receivables.

Notes Receivable

Houston Sash & Door's balance sheet has two entries for notes receivable. One represents an amount creditors incurred in the normal course of business with Houston Sash & Door. The other, Note Receivable—Officer, represents a debt Mr. Houston owes the business. This is the one to which you should give special attention. Is there an enforceable promissory note backing up the debt? Since Mr. Houston was dealing with a company he owns himself, there may not be. Since the receivable appears as a current asset, it should be payable within a year. Is it? Most important, how are you going to deal with his personal debt to the business when you buy the business? Will you require that it be paid at the closing? Will you insist on withholding part of the purchase price, in order to assure that the debt is paid when it comes due? Whatever you do, don't forget about this important item.

Pay close attention to the other notes receivable entry. Just because a note is included as a current asset doesn't mean it can be collected within a year. A note receivable may have started out in life as an account receivable. When the debtor couldn't pay, the creditor did the next best thing: The creditor had the debtor sign a short-term promissory note. But since the debtor couldn't pay the debt when it was a receivable, there's no assurance the debtor will be able to pay the promissory note either.

Inventory

If the business you're contemplating buying is a service business, you won't have inventory to worry about. But if you're thinking of buying a business that manufactures and/or distributes products, you'll be faced with the problem of valuing and dealing with the seller's inventory.

On December 31, 1985, Houston Sash & Door had $203,841 in its Inventory account. Does this mean that the inventory is *worth* $203,841 or that it could be *sold* for $203,841? Neither. Since the balance sheet records only what was *paid* for assets, it provides us with hardly a clue as to what inventory is worth or what it can be sold for, *if at all!* Mr. Houston's inventory may be worth far more than $203,841, far less, or zero. How's this possible? Very often inventory decreases in value as it sits on the shelves. If a competitor comes out with a new product, improves a product, or produces the same product for less, your inventory becomes that much less valuable. Here's a rather extreme example that proves the point: In the 1970s the federal government prohibited the sale of children's pajamas treated with the chemical TRIS. If you had a row of shelves stocked with TRIS-treated pajamas, what would your inventory be worth? Unless it had value as rags, probably zero. When inventory becomes unsaleable, or can't be sold because it's been stolen or otherwise can't be found, the business's accountants should *write down* the inventory, that is, change the figures on the balance sheet to a lower amount. But unless you're dealing with the extreme example of the government prohibiting the sale of an item, whether or not an item is unsaleable is highly subjective. An owner is not likely to write down inventory "nailed to the shelf" if a sale of the business is in the offing. It's another example of prettifying the books.

Not only doesn't the balance sheet tell you how much the inventory is worth, it doesn't tell you what it is. To an accountant inventory can exist in three "stages": as raw materials (such as Houston Sash & Door's raw lumber), as work in process (the lumber being made into windows and doors), and as finished goods (the completed windows and doors). Obviously, the value to you of raw lumber isn't as great as the value of a finished door. If all your inventory were in the form of completed doors and windows, all you would have to do is sell them. If all you had was raw lumber, you would have to incur the expense of converting the lumber into finished goods. You and your accountant should check how much of the inventory falls into each category. When we get to Chapter 11, which deals with all the steps that should be taken before a sale is closed, we'll see that one of the steps is to actually count the inventory on hand shortly before the closing.

LIFO and FIFO

We said that the balance sheet records only what was paid for assets, not what they're worth. One of the trickiest aspects of the balance sheet for a nonaccountant is the problem of what actually was paid for the inventory. Here's the problem: Houston Sash & Door buys inventory (raw lumber) throughout the year. Also throughout the year Houston Sash & Door converts the lumber to finished products and sells them. Let's assume that the cost of the lumber keeps rising during the year (a pretty good assumption in inflationary times). How do we know if the lumber on hand on December 31 was the "cheap" lumber bought on January 2, 1985, or the more expensive lumber bought on December 31, or an amalgam of all of the lumber purchases throughout the year? It's impossible to tell for sure unless you tag each item, but your intuition would tell you that it's more likely that the lumber purchased *last* is the lumber that was still around on December 31. In other words, the *first* lumber in was the *first* to go out, or FIFO (first in, first out). That's what your intuition would tell you, but accountants aren't necessarily guided by intuition. Quite the contrary. Accountants are allowed to assume that the *last* lumber which was bought was the *first* lumber sold, or LIFO (last in, first out). Does all this affect the financial statements? It does. Enormously.

If we use the LIFO method, we're saying the inventory that appears on the balance sheet is the "cheap" inventory bought on January 2. As a result, the inventory appearing on the balance sheet is lower, which makes the net worth of the business lower. If we use the FIFO method, the reverse is true; FIFO results in a higher-priced inventory and a greater net worth.

Let's take a look at the income statement on page 33. The way in which Gross Profit is computed is directly, but subtly, influenced by whether LIFO or FIFO is used. As you can see, Gross Profit is derived by subtracting Cost of Goods Sold from Sales Revenue:

Sales Revenue
— Costs of Goods Sold
———————————
= Gross Profit

Cost of Goods Sold is derived by adding the beginning inventory (the inventory on hand at the start of the year) to the cost of inventory purchased during the year and subtracting the cost of the ending inventory (the inventory on hand at the end of the year) as follows:

> Beginning Inventory
> + Purchases of Inventory during the year
> – Ending Inventory
> _____
> = Cost of Goods Sold

This means that if the ending inventory is *greater,* the cost of goods sold is *smaller*. If the cost of goods sold is smaller, gross profit is greater. In inflationary times the ending inventory will be greater if we use the FIFO method, since it assumes we counted the more expensive inventory on hand at year-end. If we use LIFO, the reverse if true: by assuming that the ''cheap'' inventory is still on hand at year-end, cost of goods sold is greater and gross profit is smaller. You can remember this with an easy rule of thumb: *In times of rising prices, LIFO understates earnings and FIFO overstates earnings.*

Is one method ''better'' than another? Even though your intuition tells you that FIFO makes more sense, LIFO may be a better predictor of earnings. As we've just seen, LIFO increases cost of goods sold, resulting in lower earnings. It's a more conservative form of accounting. The assumption is that a business's cost of goods sold *next year* will more closely approximate the conservative result LIFO produces.

From your standpoint as the buyer of a business, you should be careful about a business that reports inventory on FIFO. Not only does FIFO pump up the net worth of the business by increasing the values assigned to inventory, it also increases the business' gross profit by lowering the cost of goods sold. As we'll see in Chapter 5, the book value of the business and its earnings are the two components that go into a business's valuation. If both these components are too high, you may wind up paying too much.

Prepaid Expenses

If you pay for an item before you're obligated to, it's considered an asset, since it's the equivalent of money in your pocket when the time comes for the expense to be paid. This is usually the last current asset, since its the least likely to be converted into cash, should you need the cash.

Plant and Equipment

The big ticket items appear here. These are the fixed assets, which are not likely to be converted into cash during the business's operating cycle. The Plant and Equipment account includes all the hard assets not sold to customers, such as office furniture, machinery, cars and trucks, and equipment. It includes those items that are expected to be around for more than a year and are *depreciated,* rather than *expensed,* items. Had Houston Sash & Door owned any real estate, there would also be a Real Estate account.

We've stated that the balance sheet tells us what the business paid for the assets, not what they're worth now or what it would cost to replace them. Not only that, the Total Plant and Equipment entry is *net* of Accumulated Depreciation. On December 31, 1985, the total cost of all the items that appear in the Equipment, Furniture, and Fixtures ledgers was $60,868. Since then the owners of the business have taken $31,592 in depreciation deductions, so that the *adjusted book value* of this account is $29,276.

The problem is that since 1981, when Congress passed the Economic Recovery Tax Act, businesses have been allowed to take huge depreciation deductions in the early years of an asset's life, at the expense of lower (or no) depreciaton deductions in later years. The deductions a business can take need not, and usually do not, have any relation to the actual useful life of the asset. For example, one of Houston Sash & Door's milling machines may last for twenty years, but the business may write it off over eight years. This means that the book value of depreciable assets (which includes all business real estate but the land itself) on the balance sheet is usually grossly understated, with no relation to market value or the replacement cost of similar items.

All this means that the balance sheet doesn't tell you what the equipment is worth. Not only that, but (as we'll see in Chapter 6) if you wind up buying the owner's stock of the business, rather than the individual assets, you're going to take over the seller's depreciation schedule. The more depreciation the seller took, the less that will be available to you. The less depreciation remaining for you to use, the less will be the expenses you can report, and the higher will be your tax bill.

There's one other thing you need to be careful about when examining a business's fixed assets. If the business uses an asset but doesn't own it, it won't appear on the balance sheet. Let's assume that Houston Sash & Door uses two trucks but they're owned by Mr. Houston. When buying the business, you need to be careful to ascertain whether the owner intends to include assets that the business needs but doesn't own. If not, you're going to have to go out and buy these needed assets. The way to protect yourself is to have the seller prepare a detailed list of all the assets included in the sale. That way you won't discover after the sale that a valuable asset you thought would be part of the sale wasn't.

Accounts Payable

Just as Houston Sash & Door grants its customers credit, the people who supply Houston Sash & Door with lumber and other materials sell these items on credit. When such a credit transaction occurs, it generates an *account payable*.

When we examine Houston Sash & Door's Accounts Payable account on December 31, 1985, we note that the $65,703 it owed is rather insignificant compared to its almost $2 million in sales and is less than half of its payables as of December 31, 1984. How do we explain this? It may be that Mr. Houston, fortified with lots of cash, took advantage of cash payment discounts offered by suppliers. It also may be that business was slow toward year-end (the business may be seasonal in nature) and fewer items were purchased. There's one circumstance, however, where low (or no) accounts payable are a problem: the business's credit is so bad that no one will sell to it on credit and all purchases *must* be made COD!

Notes Payable and Long-Term Debt

We've covered this one. It may be the flip side of the owner trying to prettify the balance sheet by taking out a loan to increase the cash. It may also represent a problem if the lender has a security interest in the assets, which may prevent the assets from being sold. If a note must be prepaid within a year, it should appear as a current liability. If it doesn't have to be repaid within a year, it should appear as a long-term debt.

Paid-in Capital

What's left over after liabilities are subtracted from assets is the Net Worth of the business, which usually has two components: *Paid-in Capital* and *Retained Earnings*. The paid-in capital is what the owners contributed to the business when they started it, or put in later if the business needed more. Very often successful businesses start very small, with little invested capital. It's not at all unusual for the paid-in capital to be miniscule compared to the net worth of the business.

Let's skip over Retained Earnings. We'll discuss this item when we discuss the income statement.

THE INCOME STATEMENT

The balance sheet is a snapshot of a business as of a given moment in time. The income statement isn't. Rather, *it's a summary of everything that happened* during a given period of time. The combined income statement on page 33 shows what happened for two periods, the period from January 1, 1984, through December 31, 1984, and the period from January 1, 1985, through December 31, 1985. The moment in time of the balance sheet will always correspond to the last day of the period covered by the income statement.

We won't need to go into every item on the income statement; most are self-explanatory. Let's highlight some items that should raise red flags.

Sales Revenue

According to the income statement, Houston Sash & Door sold windows and doors totalling $1,881,117 during the period that began on January 1, 1985 and ended on December 31, 1985. Right? Not exactly.

The accountant who prepared the income statement wasn't kind enough to break out for us the *gross* amount of sales and deduct from that number the *sales returns* the business experienced. Houston Sash & Door might have actually sold $2,381,177 worth of windows and doors of which $500,000 worth was returned and not paid for. If a business has a high level of returns, it may mean that a high level of inferior goods may have been shipped. If this is true, it may mean that lawsuits can be expected from customers who bought and paid for goods and now aren't satisfied, or worse, have been injured by the goods or have had their businesses harmed by them. If you find an unusually high level of returns (which you can't find from this income statement), keep digging.

Don't forget what we learned about Accounts Receivable. In order to prettify the financial statements, the seller may have artificially increased sales by granting easy credit to unqualified customers. These sales show up as Sales Revenues on the income statement, as well as Accounts Receivable on the balance sheet, whether or not any of these sales will ultimately bring in any cash.

Rent

To review what we noted in Chapter 3: You need to examine the lease. The rent may be going up.

Professional Services

This refers to legal and accounting fees the business incurred during the period. Compare 1984 with 1985. They were miniscule in 1984 and in excess of $58,000 in 1985. If the large increase represented accounting fees, it probably means that the business experienced an IRS audit. At the present time it may be impossible to determine whether the audit resulted favorably or whether a big tax bill is coming. Not only that, the IRS may have audited only one prior year. If the accountant took the same aggressive position with respect to a certain item(s) on the tax returns for other years, you may be faced with an audit for those years as well. If the large increase in Professional Services was due to legal fees, it probably means the business was involved in a lawsuit. Keep digging.

Net Income

We'll see in Chapter 5 that the *real* income a business earns for its owners is different from the bottom line figure that appears on the income statement. The Net Income Houston Sash & Door shows for the year ending December 31, 1985, is $280,397. But this doesn't mean there's $280,397 in cash available for the owner. There may be *more*! After all, we arrived at Net Income by deducting an amount for depreciation. But you don't have to spend any money to get the depreciation deduction, the way you do to get a deduction for office supplies, utilities, and the like. The point here is that there is a critical difference between a business's Net Income and its *cash flow*. More on that later.

ANALYZING THE FINANCIAL STATEMENTS (RATIOS! RATIOS! RATIOS!)

Not only does each account need to be examined separately, but observing the interplay of the various accounts will tell us a great deal about a business's past and provide us a few clues as to its future.

1. *Liquidity Ratios.* There's nothing more important to the financial health of a business than its *liquidity,* that is, its ability to pay its bills. A business may have high sales, a big new building and a fistfull of contracts. But if it can't meet its payroll, the business is hurting. Technically, it's *insolvent.* In the depths of the Depression, President Hoover remarked that the economy was "fundamentally sound" and that things would turn around "in the long run." One wag remarked that while things might be rosy in the long run, most people need to eat every day. The same holds true for businesses.

The *working capital* of a business is the amount of liquid assets the business has available to it, measured as follows:

Current Assets − Current Liabilities = Working Capital

On December 31, 1985, Houston Sash & Door had $793,382 in current assets and $86,243 in current liabilities, or $707,139 in working capital. Considering that its annual operating expenses are only in the $500,000 range, the business is very liquid.

A better measure of liquidity is the *current ratio*, the ratio of current assets divided by current liabilities:

$$\frac{\text{Current Assets}}{\text{Current Liabilities}} = \text{current ratio}$$

Houston Sash & Door's current ratio is $707,139 divided by $86,243, or 9.2. Generally, a current ratio in excess of 2.0 is considered adequate; a current ratio between 1.0 and 1.5 is considered low. A current ratio below 1.0 may indicate that the business has difficulty paying its bills.

The problem with current ratio is that it includes inventory and prepaid expenses, items that may not be very liquid. Inventory is not as easily converted into cash in a pinch as accounts and notes receivables and certainly isn't as liquid as cash itself. For this reason, many analysts remove inventory from the computation to determine a *quick ratio:*

$$\frac{\text{Cash (+ cash equivalents)} + \text{Accounts and Notes Receivable (trade)}}{\text{Current Liabilities}} = \text{quick ratio}$$

Houston Sash & Door's quick ratio is 65, a very liquid business.

The *Sales/Accounts Receivable ratio* is a measure of how fast accounts receivable are being converted into cash. This is important because the slower that receivables are converted into cash, the greater the cash drain on the business. If receivables become cash faster, this cash can be invested and earn interest. If receivables can't be collected, the business may have to borrow money in order to pay its bills, incurring a greater interest expense. The ratio is derived by dividing net sales by trade accounts and notes receivables, as follows:

$$\frac{\text{Net Sales}}{\text{Accounts and Notes Receivable}} = \frac{\text{Sales/Accounts}}{\text{Receivables ratio}}$$

Houston Sash & Door's Sales/Accounts Receivable Ratio on December 31, 1985, was $1,881,117 divided by $291,104, or 6.5. This means that the business's accounts receivable were turning over 6.5 times during the year. The higher the ratio, the faster that accounts receivable are being turned into cash. As we'll see later (when we compare these ratios with those of other businesses), this ratio is a bit low.

We can go even further and compute the *amount of time* an average receivable is outstanding, by dividing the number of days in the year by the sales/receivables ratio:

$$\frac{365}{\text{Sales/Accounts Receivable ratio}}$$

When we do this, we find that a typical Houston Sash & Door receivable remained unpaid for fifty-six days. If we do the same computation for the period that ended on December 31, 1984, we find a sales/accounts receivable ratio of 8.7. We also find that in 1984 the average receivable remained outstanding for only forty-two days. What does this mean? It may mean nothing more than that the business generated a big new customer who demanded, and was granted, easier credit terms. But it may also mean that management has grown lax in its credit and collection policies and efforts. Worse, it may mean that inferior goods have been shipped, in order to pump up the financial statements, and the customers are refusing to pay.

For those businesses that stock inventory, a key liquidity ratio is the ratio of *Cost of Goods Sold to Inventory*. This ratio measures the number of times during the year that inventory turns over, as follows:

$$\frac{\text{Cost of Goods Sold}}{\text{Inventory}} = \text{Cost of Goods Sold/Inventory ratio}$$

A high ratio means that inventory is turning over quickly. A low ratio means that the inventory, or some line of inventory, isn't moving. This may indicate that certain lines are obsolete or that management has been overstocking. Houston Sash & Door's ratio for the period ending December 31, 1985, was $961,330 divided by $203,841, or 4.7. As we'll see, this ratio is a bit low. As with the Sales/Accounts Receivable ratio, it's possible to pinpoint the time an average item of inventory sat on the shelf by dividing the ratio into the number of days in the year:

$$\frac{365}{\text{Cost of Goods Sold/Inventory ratio}}$$

By dividing 4.7 into 365, we find a typical item in Houston Sash & Door's inventory took 77.6 days to sell.

2. *Lending Ratios.* If you're planning on buying a business and expanding it, you may need to borrow money. If the business you're buying has already borrowed, you'll have to pay that debt as well. It's important to look at your business from a lender's standpoint, since a lender wants to ascertain the same thing you do: How sound is the business?

The *EBIT/Interest Expense* ratio measures a business's earnings before interest and taxes compared with its annual interest expense, as follows:

$$\frac{\text{Earnings before Interest and Taxes (EBIT)}}{\text{Annual Interest Expense}} = \text{EBIT/Interest Expense ratio}$$

If this ratio is high, it means the business should have no problem meeting its current interest expense, which means a lender will be more easily convinced to loan the business more money. Houston Sash & Door's EBIT for 1985 was $367,037 (Net Income of

$280,397 but adding back $81,620 in taxes and $5,020 in interest.) Its interest expense was only $5,020, for a ratio of 73! No one will have any trouble lending Houston Sash & Door all the money it wants.

All lenders know, however, that the interest isn't the only element of a debt that needs to be repaid; the *principal* has to be repaid, and that part doesn't show up on the income statement, since it isn't deductible. The *Cash Flow/Current Maturities ratio* measures the cash that will be on hand to service the principal of the debt, as follows:

$$\frac{\text{Net Profits} = \text{Depreciation (and Depletion and Amortization)}}{\text{Current Portion of Long-Term Debt}} = \frac{\text{Cash Flow/Current}}{\text{Maturities ratio}}$$

Why did we add depreciation (and depletion, if we're in the oil business, or amortization of amortizable items such as noncompetition agreements) to Net Profits? Because here we're not interested in paper profits; we're interested in cash flow. Depreciation lowers our profits on paper, without a cash outlay. So we add that back. The Current Portion of Long-Term Debt represents the principal of the debts that will have to be paid within the next year. We know that Houston Sash & Door has long term debt of $45,000, but we don't know, at least from the balance sheet, how much of it comes due in the coming year. Let's assume half of it does, or $22,500. The cash flow/current maturities ratio is computed as follows:

$$\frac{\begin{array}{c}\$280,397 \text{ (net profit)} \\ + \ \$9,365 \text{ (depreciation)}\end{array}}{\$22,500} \quad \frac{\$289,762}{\$22,500} = 12.9$$

The higher the ratio, easier it is to service the principal as it comes due. Once again, no one is going to have any problem loaning money to Houston Sash & Door.

A very important consideration to a lender (and to a buyer) is the extent to which a business is *leveraged*, that is, how much has the business borrowed compared with what it's worth? A highly leveraged business is inherently less flexible than a business that has borrowed less. Not only will it be less able to borrow more money, it will be less able to weather downturns in business, because of the fixed nature of its interest and principal costs. The *Debt/Net Worth ratio* compares total liabilities and net worth, as follows:

$$\frac{\text{Total Liabilities}}{\text{Tangible Net Worth}} = \text{Liabilities/Net Worth ratio}$$

We use only the tangible Net Worth here. If a business has certain intangible assets, such as goodwill, on its balance sheet, we back that number out. The higher the ratio, the more leverage the business has and the less likely it will be to borrow money. Houston Sash & Door's Liabilities/Net Worth ratio is $131,243, divided by $691,415, or .18! This business is hardly leveraged at all.

3. *A Key Management Ratio.* We haven't covered all of the possible ratios we can employ in any business. There's one, however, that should be highlighted, because it goes to the heart of how well a business is doing. The *Profit/Assets ratio* measures how effectively the business converts invested capital into profits. If you're buying a business, you're buying assets, in the hope of turning these assets into earnings. You'd do the same by buying an asset such as a certificate of deposit and having that asset produce interest earnings. Presumably, the business you buy will be able to generate greater earnings than a certificate of deposit. The Profit/Assets ratio compares profits before taxes with total assets. Since we don't want the ratio to be distorted by the vagaries of changing tax rates, we use profit before taxes. Since this ratio is expressed as a percentage, the ratio is multiplied by 100, as follows:

$$\frac{\text{Profit before Taxes}}{\text{Total Assets}} \times 100 = \text{Profit/Assets percentage}$$

The higher the percentage, the more capable the business is of turning invested capital into earnings. This is one ratio that can produce a *negative* figure if the business has no profits and is losing money. Houston Sash & Door's Profit/Assets Percentage is as follows:

$$\frac{\$362,017 \text{ (Net Profit before Taxes)}}{\$822,658 \text{ (Total Assets)}} \times 100 = 44\%$$

COMPARING THE RATIOS WITH COMPARABLE BUSINESSES

Now that we've determined the ratios, what do we do with them? Standing alone, they provide a pretty good idea of how the business stacks up, how healthy or troubled it is. By using the ratios we derive from a given year's balance sheet and income statement, we can compare the results with that same business's financial statements for prior years and determine the financial *trends* for the business. An important point is worth noting here: Even though we've reviewed Houston Sash & Door's financial statements for two annual periods, we don't have enough to establish any consistent trends; to do this, we should have as many as five years to work with. If the business you're contemplating buying has been around for as many as five years, get the financial statements for all these years and compare them.

But we can go even further. We can compare Houston Sash & Door's ratios with those of other similar businesses. How do we do this? Fortunately, we have help. There're two excellent source books: *Industry Norms and Key Business Ratios,* published by Dun & Bradstreet, and *Annual Statement Studies,* published by Robert Morris Associates. Both books can be found in most public libraries. If you're working with a good business broker, the broker will have one or both of these books. (If the broker doesn't, it should tell you something about the quality of the broker you're dealing with.) Various trade associations also compile the relevant ratios for the businesses who are members of their association.

If you turn to *Annual Statement Studies* or *Industry Norms and Key Business Ratios,* you'll find each has a page devoted to the type of business you're interested in. *Annual Statement Studies* has a page headed "Manufacturers—Millwork." Not only does it list the ratios for all the businesses engaged in millwork, it breaks the listing down by size of business, grouped by total assets. It also provides a breakdown of the results according to the median of all millwork businesses and according to those that fell on the high and low end of the scale. Let's take a look at the breakdown of current ratio:

0–$1 Million	$1 Million–$10 Million	$10 Million–$50 Million
2.3	2.6	2.3
1.6	1.6	1.8
1.2	1.3	1.1

Since Houston Sash & Door's total assets are under $1 million, we'd look in the column that reports businesses in that range. We find that for businesses of this size, the median current ratio is 1.6 The current ratio of 2.3 represents the half-way point of all those above the median, and 1.2 represents the half-way point of all of those below the median. Houston Sash & Door's current ratio is 9.2, indicating it's far more liquid than most similar businesses.

Let's take a look at the Sales/Receivables ratios for comparable businesses:

0–$1 Million		$1 Million–$10 Million		$10 Million–$50 Million	
(31)	11.8	(30)	12.1	(30)	12.1
(45)	8.1	(39)	9.4	(43)	8.4
(59)	6.2	(49)	7.4	(49)	7.5

This table shows not only what the median ratios are, but in parentheses the average number of days the receivables were outstanding. The median Sales/Receivables ratio for a millwork business having assets under $1 million is 8.1. Houston Sash & Door's ratio for 1985 was 6.5, placing it slightly below the industry norm. Its average receivable was collected in fifty-six days, also slightly below the norm.

As you can see, you can compare any of the ratios of the business you are evaluating with those of comparable businesses. And not only that, if you get your hands on the financial statements from prior years and chart a trend, you'll be able to chart the *trends* of similar businesses, since the ratios of other businesses from prior years are also reported.

Comparing the financial statements of the target business with other businesses may show you that the target is in pretty good shape. Does this mean there's a certainty the business will do just as well after you buy it as before? Of course not. New products, foreign or domestic competition, uncontrollable economic conditions, and a host of other variables may turn the business upside down. If the business is already upside down, your energy or ability may turn the business around. Analzying the financial statements provides guidance, not conclusions.

Does an analysis of the financial statements tell us how much we should pay for the business and on what terms? It leads us there, that's all. As you'll see next, valuing the businesses and determining how much you want to pay is the toughest job of all.

Chapter **5**

NEGOTIATING THE SALE (I): HOW MUCH WILL I PAY AND WHEN?

Now comes the hard part: determining how much you'll pay for the business and on what terms. By the time you get this far, you may have decided you *really* want this business. You may already be imagining what it will be like to run it. You've probably pictured what owning the business will feel like compared with your present job or business. You may already have gone so far as to plan some changes you'll make or some new directions in which you'll take the business.

SOME PRELIMINARY POINTERS

Slow down! The decision you make should be an *informed* decision, not one that's the result of a passion blinding your reason. Here are a few pointers that will prevent you from making a mistake.

1. *Never Make the Opening Bid.* "What'll you give me for my business?" There's no answer to that question, or at least shouldn't be. For starters, if you think the business is worth $1,000,000 and the seller is willing to sell it for $800,000, you can rest assured you'll wind up paying $1,000,000 if you tell the seller that's what it's worth. Always try to smoke out the asking price first. If the business has been listed with a business broker, the broker will know at least what the initial asking price is.

If the asking price is ridiculously high, you still should refrain from making an opening bid. The high asking price may be little more than a gambit to get you to make an offer. If you make an offer after receiving an absurdly high asking price, you're still negotiating against yourself.

A high asking price often reflects what a seller really thinks the business is worth. Sellers often think their businesses are worth far more than they are. If the seller has listed the business with an inexperienced or incompetent broker, the broker may have put stars in the seller's eyes about what the broker can get for the business. If that's the case, it'll make buying the business at a decent price that much more difficult.

2. *Don't Let on How Eager You Are.* No matter how much you want this business, keep a poker face! If the seller learns you're dying to get in, the terms will stiffen. Above all, resist high-pressure tactics. The seller may tell you there're three other people looking at the business and that the first one who forks over a down payment will get the deal. The seller may or may not be telling the truth. Even if it is the truth, let the others make a snap decision if they wish.

3. *Never Make an Offer before Conducting a Complete Investigation.* Let's say the seller quotes you a price that sounds fairly reasonable. You may, ultimately, be willing to pay this price. But if you agree to the price (and the terms) early on, the price and the terms tend to become fixed in stone. There's no chance you're going to wind up paying *more* than the agreed-upon price; if the terms remain fluid, you may wind up paying less.

Don't agree on the price or the terms until you, your attorney, and your accountant have had a chance to conduct a thorough investigation. If you later find there are skeletons you didn't know about, the negative things you find may result in a lower price or better terms. But this won't happen if you and the seller have already agreed on a price. There's nothing that frustates an attorney more than having a client who has already agreed on all the terms of a sale and who shows up the day before the scheduled closing asking the attorney to "review all the paperwork." If that review reveals assets tied up by UCC-1 filings, leases about to expire, or any of a host of other problems, having already agreed to the terms is going to make it that much more difficult to cut a better deal. If the seller offers you what sounds like good terms, your response should be along these lines: "Your offer sounds good, but I just don't know. I'll have to have it reviewed by my attorney or accountant. There're a few things they'll have to check before I can give my OK." At that point start your investigation.

4. *Conduct the Negotiations Secretly.* This is one point the seller will readily accede to, because it's in the seller's interest, as well as the buyer's, to conduct the negotiations secretly. In the early stages this means not letting the employees in on the fact a sale is in the offering. As we saw earlier, if they know that a sale is pending, it may affect their morale—they may even start job hunting. If customers find out that the business is being sold, they may figure that the disruption inherent in a sale is a good opportunity to hold off paying their debts. The seller doesn't want to harm his own business by conducting public negotiations; the sale may fall through. In your turn, you don't want the disclosure of negotiations to harm the business should you ultimately buy.

All this simply means that negotiations shouldn't be conducted at the business during working hours. By conducting negotiations at the business, you'll have ready access to the business's books, ledgers, contracts, leases, and any other documents. If the seller needs to demonstrate a procedure for you, the seller will be able to. By negotiating on site after hours you'll be able to negotiate the sale away from the prying eyes of employees and customers and other outsiders who don't need to know about the sale until it happens.

PREPARE THAT PRO FORMA

Prior to making an offer to buy (or even making a final decision whether to buy) you should prepare a *cash flow projection,* estimating what the sources of cash and the cash needs of the business will be. The cash flow projection is usually called the *pro forma,* or the "pro forma P and L."

There're two very good reasons for preparing a pro forma: You'll need it, and your banker will require it. You'll need it because no matter what fancy footwork your accountant can accomplish, keeping a business going ultimately boils down to how much cash is in the till. If you don't plan and two years down the road there's no cash, you're in big trouble. This is why lenders won't lend you any money unless they've had the opportunity to eyeball your pro forma very carefully. Even if you don't need to borrow any money to buy a business, you still should prepare the pro forma. There're few absolutes contained in this book, but here's one: *Anyone who buys a business without first preparing a pro forma is crazy!*

Let's go back to Houston Sash & Door's combined income statement (page 33). One thing about it should be readily apparent: It doesn't contain enough information with which to plan. Having two years' worth of financial information is better than having only one, but we'll soon see it's not enough with which to make any meaningful projections.

Let's assume that you and your accountant have obtained *five years'* financial statements from Mr. Houston. Your accountant should then summarize most of the relevant information on a one-page spread sheet. Study the one on pages 64 and 65 for a few minutes.

You can immediately see that the spread sheet doesn't contain all the entries on the income statement (page 33). The Salary—Officer and Travel and Entertainment entries don't appear. The reason is that the $100,000 annual salary paid to Mr. Houston doesn't represent a cost of doing business. We've also assumed that in talking to Mr. Houston you learned that the Travel and Entertainment entry really amounts to nothing more than the vacations, parties, and country club dues Mr. and Mrs. Houston incur annually; they're really not business expenses. Mr. Houston may have a problem justifying these expenses to the IRS. Whether or not he can get them past the tax collectors, they don't represent a cost of doing business and will disappear, when Mr. Houston retires to Spain. Later on we'll plug in a salary for you on the pro forma. We'll also give you an allowance for *real* business travel and entertainment. But for now we just want to determine the real cost of doing business, so we can estimate what it will be.

As you can see, the accountant has also computed the percentage increase for each item over the five-year period and has divided the result by 5 to determine the average annual increase for most items.

Let's take a closer look at each item. For most of the items, we'll make certain assumptions about why the numbers are as they are.

1. *Gross Profit.* As you'll recall from Chapter 4, annual gross profit is the result of subtracting the cost of the goods sold from the total price charged to the customers. Over a five-year period sales rose at an average of 2.8 percent per year. But let's look a little more carefully: Sales rose from $1,832,286 in 1984 to only $1,881,117 in 1985, an increase of only 2.5 percent. We also saw that the length of time accounts receivable were uncollected increased from 1984 to 1985, as did the time inventory sat on the shelf. Did Mr. Houston artificially pump up sales in order to keep sales for 1985 consistent with prior years? Hard to tell. At any rate, you may be better off assuming sales will increase at an annual rate of 2.5 percent, rather than 2.8 percent.

We can also see that the Cost of Goods Sold (in our example, the price of lumber) has increased very modestly: an average of only 0.6 percent a year. This modest increase has been largely responsible for the 5.2 percent annual increase in Gross Profit.

2. *Labor Costs.* As a business owner you'll be concerned about the total cost of labor, as well as the cost of each item. By grouping all labor costs together, we see that the total cost has increased an average of 5.8 percent per year. But wait! Salary expense, which grew fairly steadily from 1981 to 1984, increased from $137,461 in 1984 to $168,702 in 1985, an 18.5 percent increase! Why? Let's assume that Mr. Houston tells you, and you confirm, that the sudden increase resulted from Mr. Houston's son, who used to work for minimal wages, having joined the army. He had to be replaced with someone who gets paid at the going rate. That's a good sign, since it means that wages in the industry are not increasing more steeply than in the past.

There's an "error" in the computation of the increase in labor costs. Even though bonuses have technically increased by 5.5 percent annually, Mr. Houston began giving them as late as 1983.

HOUSTON SASH & DOOR, INC.
Five-Year Income Statements

	1985	1984	1983	1982	1981	Five-Year Increase (%)	Annual Increase (%)
Sales Revenue	$1,881,117	$1,832,286	$1,699,812	$1,614,930	$1,612,330	14.2	2.8
Cost of Goods Sold	961,330	952,557	948,112	939,010	931,828	3.0	0.6
Gross Profit	$ 919,787	$ 879,729	$ 751,700	$ 675,920	$ 680,502	25.0	5.0
Labor Costs							
Salary	168,702	137,461	131,400	122,833	118,996	29.4	5.8
Bonuses	1,842	1,500	1,330	—	—	27.8	5.5
Taxes, Payroll	17,188	15,390	15,002	14,555	13,977	18.7	3.7
Subtotal	$ 187,732	$ 154,351	$ 147,732	$ 137,488	$ 132,973	29.1	5.8
Operating Expenses							
Advertising	8,920	8,550	7,241	6,900	—	22.6	4.5
Rent and Building	55,753	55,753	55,753	55,753	55,753	0	0

Utilities	27,139	26,333	25,546	24,510	23,690	12.7	2.5
Insurance, General	11,100	11,100	9,610	9,610	8,740	21.2	4.2
Telephone	10,958	8,752	8,012	7,468	6,999	36.1	7.2
Office Supplies	31,943	28,466	37,466	26,141	40,050	—	—
Professional Services	58,300	980	4,187	770	1,141	—	—
Miscellaneous	320	39	5,640	182	940	—	6.5
Subtotal	$ 204,433	$ 139,973	$ 153,455	$ 131,334	$ 137,313	32.8	
Total	$ 392,165	$ 294,324	$ 301,187	$ 268,822	$ 270,286	37.0	7.4
Other Expenses							
Depreciation	9,365	10,891	11,411	13,870	14,800	—	—
Interest	5,020	1,122	1,440	1,179	1,990	—	—
Federal and State Income Taxes	81,620	82,770	79,550	74,340	75,181	7.8	1.5
Net Adjusted Income	$ 296,160	$ 199,541	$ 208,786	$ 179,433	$ 178,315	39.8	7.9

Since then, employees' bonus costs have increased 27.8 percent annually. Let's assume that Mr. Houston tells you his competitors grant high bonuses and he's had to increase them to catch up. After you buy the business, your bonus costs may also rise rapidly. Let's assume they rise at the same rate they increased from 1984 to 1985, or 18.5 percent.

3. *Advertising.* The same holds true for advertising costs. Over the five-year period advertising costs rose at an annual rate of 4.5 percent; however, they've risen at an annual rate of 5.7 percent ever since Mr. Houston felt he had to start advertising. These costs are more likely to keep rising at the higher rate.

4. *Rent and Building.* The rent hasn't changed over five years and is obviously fixed. But every lease expires, and it's probable the rent will increase when the lease runs out. If the lease is about to expire, it's imperative to try to find out what the rent will be. Let's assume that the lease expires on December 31, 1986. Let's also assume that the landlord tells you any new lease will increase the fixed rent by 15 percent and will include an annual increase equal to the annual increase in the consumer price index (CPI). This means you're going to have to estimate what the CPI increase will be. If we assume a 5 percent annual increase starting in 1988, the annual rent will be as follows:

1986	1987	1988	1989	1990
$55,753	$64,116	$67,321	$70,687	$74,222

5. *Utilities, Insurance, and Telephone.* These items appear to increase annually, probably from increases in costs. Note, however, that insurance costs increase every *two* years; the next increase may not be until 1987.

6. *Office Supplies, Professional Services, and Miscellaneous.* These items don't increase or decrease in any predictable way. Each year appears to produce its own costs. With Office Supplies it's possible to determine an *average* ($32,813) and assume future increases based it. As you can see, there're extraordinary items included in Professional Services for 1983 and 1985, probably IRS audits or

lawsuits. The same holds true of Miscellaneous. With both these items, it's important to determine the cause of the extraordinary items, to determine whether they're likely to recur.

The information we've obtained from the financial statements for the five preceding years represents most of the input for the pro forma. Most, but not all. Mr. Houston paid himself a salary in all the years he ran Houston Sash & Door. You're going to want to pay yourself a salary as well. You may be satisfied, at least at the start, with a salary not as great as the $100,000 Mr. Houston took every year. You may be satisfied with $50,000. Let's also keep an amount reserved for *real* business travel and entertainment. Being new to the business, you may well incur expenses in visiting present customers and suppliers or generating new ones.

In preparing the pro forma, you should estimate *conservatively*. That means erring on the low side when estimating sales and erring on the high side when estimating expenses. It also means anticipating and providing for expenses your seller didn't have. For example, Houston Sash & Door's income statement makes no provision for the purchases of furniture and equipment. That's because these items, being nondeductible, aren't included in the income statement. But buying these items will cost you money. If you're planning on buying capital items on credit, you'll have to make assumptions as to the credit terms you'll get.

Keep the pro forma *simple*. It should have all the supporting documentation you can muster, but the *summary page* of the pro forma should be clear and concise, preferably one page. Remember, the difference between an understandable pro forma and a confusing one can be the difference between getting a loan and not getting one. If the pro forma is confusing to a banker, it's likely to be confusing to you. A pro forma that doesn't educate is no good to anyone. With this in mind, let's turn to the pro forma for Houston Sash & Door for the next five years, which appears on page 68.

ANALYZING YOUR OWN PRO FORMA

Now that we've prepared the pro forma, let's see what we've got. First of all, will any of the numbers on the pro forma prove to be

HOUSTON SASH & DOOR, INC.
Pro Forma Income and Expenses: 1986–1990

	1986	1987	1988	1989	1990
Sales Revenue (2.5%)	$1,928,145	$1,976,348	$2,025,757	$2,076,401	$2,128,311
Cost of Goods Sold (.6%)	967,098	972,900	978,737	984,609	990,516
Gross Profit	$ 961,047	$1,003,448	$1,047,020	$1,091,792	$1,137,795
Operating Expenses					
Labor Costs					
Salary Expense (6%)	178,824	189,553	200,926	212,982	225,761
Bonuses (18.5%)	2,182	2,586	3,065	3,632	4,304
Taxes, Payroll (3.7%)	17,823	18,483	19,167	19,876	20,611
	$ 198,829	$ 210,622	$ 223,158	$ 236,490	$ 250,676
Advertising (5.7%)	9,428	9,965	10,533	11,134	11,769
Rent (15% + CPI)	55,753	64,116	67,321	70,687	74,222
Utilities (2.5%)	27,817	28,512	29,225	29,956	30,705
Insurance (4.2%)	11,566	12,051	12,557	13,085	13,634
Telephone (7.2%)	11,746	12,592	13,499	14,471	15,513
Office Supplies (average + 6%)	34,781	36,868	39,080	41,425	43,911
Professional Services					
(adjusted average + 6%)	1,875	1,988	2,107	2,233	2,367
Miscellaneous					
(adjusted average + 6%)	392	416	440	467	495
	$ 352,187	$ 377,130	$ 397,920	$ 419,948	$ 443,292
Equipment	10,000	4,000	4,000	4,000	44,000
Federal and State Taxes	71,883	74,991	76,881	78,440	79,211
Net Income (before interest)	$ 526,977	$ 547,327	$ 568,219	$ 589,404	$ 571,292

accurate? Not likely. They're all *assumptions,* our best guess of what the future will bring, based on past performance. Let's review the assumptions. The numbers in parentheses represent the percentage annual increase we've assumed, again based on past history. For the Rent entry we've used an assumption based on our negotiations with the landlord: a 15 percent annual increase starting in 1987 plus an annual increase based on the CPI, which we've assumed will be 6 percent. Of course, if the CPI turns out to be higher, rental expense will go up. We've taken an average figure for office supplies and increased the average by 6 percent. We've taken an *adjusted average* for Professional Services and Miscellaneous; that is, we've thrown out the years that had extraordinary items and averaged the remaining years, increasing the result annually by 6 percent.

We've determined we may have some expenses our seller didn't have. We've assumed we'll have to discard an aging piece of equipment and replace it with an item we believe will cost $50,000. Let's also assume we believe we can buy the equipment for $10,000 down and pay the remaining $40,000 on a promissory note. For the sake of simplicity, we've assumed that the note will be payable interest only at a rate of 10 percent until 1990, when the entire note will come due. The repayment of the principal would never appear on the income statements, since its a nondeductible income. Here we're considering only the influx and outgo of cash.

We have an entry called Depreciation in the income statement, but we don't on the pro forma. Even though it's an item of expense for accounting purposes, it *increases* cash to the extent it *reduces* federal and state taxes. We've assumed your accountant has computed the effect of the purchase of the equipment on the estimated taxes the business will have to pay.

At this point it's possible to play with the numbers. We've assumed that the cost of lumber will continue to increase at the same very low rate. Let's change this assumption and assume that lumber increases at an annual rate of 4 percent, instead of 0.6 percent. At 4 percent, Cost of Goods Sold increases as follows:

1986	1987	1988	1989	1990
$999,783	$1,039,774	$1,081,365	$1,124,620	$1,169,604

and Gross Profit decreases as follows:

1986	1987	1988	1989	1990
$928,362	$936,574	$944,392	$951,781	$958,707

By changing this single assumption, Gross Profit in 1990 has decreased by $179,088!

With the aid of a personal computer, it's easy to change assumptions and see the results instantly. There are numerous software packages on the market designed to help you prepare and "play" with your pro forma. Most accountants own or have access to this type of software.

Have we omitted anything from the pro forma? You bet we have! We've omitted the one big expense you'll have that the seller didn't: the debt you'll incur to the seller when you buy the business. *One of the principal purposes of the pro forma is to determine how much debt you can afford to pay.*

At this point we don't know how much we're going to have to pay for this business. Right now, however, all we need to know is how much we can *afford* to pay. Let's assume that you agree to buy Houston Sash & Door for $1,200,000, paying $200,000 down and $1,000,000 on a promissory note. Your pro forma will tell you how much debt you can comfortably incur and on what terms. If the note requires you to pay principal and interest at a constant rate (*ratably*) at 10 percent for ten years, your annual debt will amount to $158,581. If the seller wants the note to be paid over seven years at 11 percent, the annual bill will be $205,470. If the seller holds out for 13 percent over five years, your payments will be $273,037!* If we plug in the assumption that cost of goods sold will increase annually by 4 percent, we have to subtract $179,088

---

*You can verify this by buying a book of mortgage payment tables or a pocket calculator programmed with the tables. One of these is good to own if you're going to buy a business.

from profits in 1990. If this assumption holds true, we may not be able to afford to pay a five-year note at 13 percent. (Remember, we still haven't included your own salary. As a business owner you get paid last.) How do you estimate what kind of debt you can afford? *Only by preparing a pro forma.*

HOW TO VALUE THE SELLER'S BUSINESS

Let's assume that you, your accountant and your attorney have conducted as diligent an investigation as possible of Houston Sash & Door. Your accountant has analyzed the financial statements for the business's five preceding years, has compared them with the business's accounting ledgers, and has even sampled the invoices and check registers to verify their accuracy. The accountant has prepared a number of detailed pro formas for you that provide you with good estimates of the future of the business based on a number of assumptions. Your attorney has reviewed the leases, contracts, and loan agreements and has conducted a UCC-1 search at the secretary of state. So far, everything's a go.

Up until now we've been waltzing around the central issue: What's the business worth? Unfortunately, not only is this the key question, it's the one most difficult to answer. There're hundreds of answers, and no answers. The best you can ever do is educate yourself in the criteria that go into valuing a business and hope the result is palatable to you and leads to a sale.

There's one good rule of thumb: *There're no rules of thumb!* Anyone who tries to tell you he or she knows of a good rule of thumb for valuing a particular business is kidding you, and a lot of sellers or brokers will try to kid you. You can teach a parrot to say "A service business sells for one times annual earnings." But a parrot can't think. People who use rules of thumb are attempting to substitute slogans for thinking. Every now and then a rule of thumb will turn out to be "accurate," but when it does it's purely by chance. Even a stopped clock is accurate twice a day.

1. *"What Am I Valuing?"* (or *"What Am I Paying For?"*) The starting point in any valuation is to determine just what it is you're attempting to value. When you think of it, most sellers

really have only two things to sell: assets and the ability of these assets to produce earnings. If all a business had to sell was the first component, the assets, valuing the business would be easy. We could hire an appraiser or hold an auction. Some businesses, such as those in liquidation or those that lose money, really don't have anything to sell except their *net assets,* that is, the value of the assets after the debts have been paid. This simple calculation is sometimes referred to as *liquidation value.* Liquidation value is of little concern to you if you're buying a money-making business.

The ability of a business to use its assets to create earnings is its *goodwill.* The term *goodwill* is one of the world's worst misnomers. It has little to do with a business's reputation or standing in the community or the regard its customers hold for it. Goodwill is simply the value of the business in excess of the value of the assets. Goodwill is itself an asset, albeit an intangible one, that can be bought, sold, and valued. With many businesses it's not difficult to determine the source of the goodwill. The ability to generate earnings may result from other intangible assets such as patents, well-known trademarks, licenses, lists of customers, or profit-generating contracts. Many of these intangible assets are freely transferable; others are not. The sources of goodwill in an accounting practice may be the special skill of the owner and his list of clients. The client list may be transferable, but the owner's special skill (or personality) probably can't be transferred. Most buyers sense that an important earnings-producing element can't be transferred. If you can't transfer the goodwill, the risk to the owner is higher and the purchase price will be lower. For this reason, all other things being equal, service businesses sell for less than businesses that produce or distribute products.

It isn't quite accurate to state that goodwill represents the ability of assets to generate earnings. Any asset can generate earnings. If you took the assets of a money-losing business and sold them at an auction and invested the cash, the cash would earn something. What goodwill really represents is the ability of the assets to produce earnings *in excess* of what they otherwise would earn. Goodwill, therefore, is a measure of a business's ability to generate *excess earnings.*

When you buy a business you're buying two things: assets and the excess earnings capacity inherent in these assets, which is the goodwill. It's these two items we'll have to value in order to value the business as a whole.

2. *A Few Words from the IRS.* As with most aspects of life in the United States, the IRS has had a few words to say about the valuation of businesses. In 1959 the IRS issued Revenue Ruling 59-60. A revenue ruling doesn't carry the force of law, but it comes close. It represents the IRS's thinking on a matter having an impact on tax collection. If you disagree with them, they'll be happy to meet you in Tax Court.

The IRS is keenly interested in the value placed on the stock of a business. If an owner dies, the owner's stock may be subject to estate taxes. How much tax is due depends on the value of the stock at the time of death. The same holds true for *gift* taxes. If someone makes a gift of stock, there may be a gift tax. The extent of the tax depends on the stock's value. These concerns prompted the IRS to issue Revenue Ruling 59-60.

Revenue Ruling 59-60 doesn't concern itself with the valuation of a business for purposes of purchases and sales. Nonetheless, many business brokers and appraisers use it as a benchmark when valuing a business being sold.

Revenue Ruling 59-60 begins by defining the "fair market value" of a business. According to the IRS, the fair market value of any business is the price a willing buyer would pay and a willing seller would accept if the buyer possessed all the relevant information about the seller's business and the seller was not under any compulsion to sell. This sounds rather theoretical, and it is, but makes an important point. You can have a thousand appraisers, all of whom have postgraduate degrees, telling you a business is worth a certain amount. But if there're no buyers willing to pay that much, it isn't worth that much. If you come along and offer to pay 10 percent less and the seller accepts the offer, the price you offer and the seller accepts becomes the fair market value of the business.

The next point Revenue Ruling 59-60 makes is that there is no formula for determining what a business is worth. In other words, the IRS isn't interested in and won't listen to rules of thumb like "A liquor store is worth 14 times monthly gross." Instead, the IRS suggests that the following criteria be used when valuing a business.

(*a*) *The nature and history of the business.* Have earnings risen steadily or been unstable, rising in some years and falling in others? Does the business sell only one product or is it diversified? Diversified businesses are inherently less risky than those that depend on the sale of one product or service. Also, it's obvious a business that has experienced profits over many years is more likely to continue to produce profits than one that has been recently formed.

(*b*) *The economic outlook in general and the specific industry in particular.* Two identical businesses may have radically differing prospects if one is located in a "rust belt" city experiencing a declining population and the other is located in a boom town. Two similar businesses will have different futures if one is in an industry characterized by increasing competition and unstable prices and the other has a geographical or product monopoly. Certain businesses rely more on the managerial ability of a principal owner than do others. All these factors need to be considered.

(*c*) *Book value, financial condition, and earning capacity.* The IRS is telling you to do what we did at length in Chapter 4: Carefully examine the balance sheets and income statements for the business for the five preceding years.

(*d*) *Dividend-paying capacity.* Small businesses generally don't pay dividends, because dividends are nondeductible for tax purposes. Instead, management withdraws earnings in the form of salary, bonuses, and fringe benefits and in other ways that are deductible. The inquiry here is whether the business *could have* declared dividends even after reasonable salaries had been paid and a reasonable amount had been salted away for future expansion.

(*e*) *Does the business have some intangible value?* The focus here is on the value, if any, to be placed on such intangible factors as an advantageous location, an identifiable brand name, and the prestige of the business. Sounds a lot like goodwill, doesn't it? It is.

(*f*) *Prior sales of the company's stock.* If someone recently bought a block of the stock of the company you're valuing, this is obviously a good indicator of what the stock is worth. Just as obviously, the recent sale of a block of stock from an owner to his son isn't much help. The recent sale must have been at arm's length, that is, among unrelated parties, to be considered.

(*g*) *Market price of similar businesses.* This criterion comes last because it'll probably help least. Here the IRS is telling you to look at the quoted prices of similar businesses for which stock is listed on an exchange or traded over the counter. If a company's stock is listed, it's possible to compute a ''price earnings ratio'' and determine from the result how much confidence the public has in the company. But you're not likely to find listed companies of comparable size or geographically located near the business you're valuing. Any comparison is not likely to hold up.

Does this list get you any closer to placing a value on the business you're interested in? Maybe; maybe not. But the IRS went further and in 1968 issued Revenue Ruling 68-609, which was designed to amplify Revenue Ruling 59-60. Revenue Ruling 68-609 does provide a *formula* for valuing the earning capacity of a business in excess of the tangible assets (i.e., the *goodwill*). It recognizes what we noted previously: When you buy a business you're buying two things: tangible assets and the ability of those assets to produce profits. But the IRS really hates formulas. The IRS says in Revenue Ruling 68-609 you should use a formula only when the criteria described in Revenue Ruling 59-60 don't bring you any closer to fixing a value.

Here's the formula the IRS suggests you use:

Step 1: Determine the average annual return on the *tangible assets*. The average should be for a period of not less than five years. If no average is available, use a return of from 8 to 10 percent.

Step 2: Determine the average earnings of the business for the preceding five-year period.

Step 3: Subtract the result from step 1 from the result in step 2.

The remainder should reflect the earnings over the five-year period attributable to the intangibles, that is, the goodwill.

Step 4: Capitalize the result in step 3 by a percentage. If the business is considered a high-risk business, the percentage you plug in should be from 10 to 20 percent. If the business is low risk, plug in a percentage from 8 to 15 percent.

Step 5: Add the result from step 4 to the book value of the assets. That's the value of the business, based on the formula.

Confused? You ought to be. The reason you ought to be is that we haven't yet described the concept of *capitalization rates,* or in the lingo of the trade, *cap rates.* The cap rate is the percentage that has to be plugged in at Step 4. Plugging in the appropriate "cap rate" is the key to any valuation formula. It's what makes valuing a business so difficult.

A cap rate is based on the sound theory that the value of a future stream of income isn't the same as the value of a sum of money in hand. Think of it this way: What would you rather have, a $1,000 bill right now or $100 a year for the next ten years? Obviously the $1,000 bill is worth more, even though $100 a year also will equal $1,000. The $1,000 will earn interest for you over the ten-year period; it may be worth in excess of $2,000 after ten years. When you think of it, when you buy a business you're putting down a certain amount of money for a future income stream.

The second sound theory underlying cap rates is that a riskier income stream will command a higher rate of return and a less risky income stream will command a lower rate of return. This makes sense. You'd accept a lower rate of return from a U.S. Treasury bill sooner than you would from a bond issued by a shaky company, or any company, since no company's viability is considered as certain as that of the United States of America. But risk isn't the only element. If you think the future stream of income will be less, you'll pay less. You might part with a $500 bill for a future stream of income of $100 a year. If you thought that the income stream would amount to only $90 a year, you might be willing to part with only $400. You might be willing to part with even less if you thought there was a high risk in your actually receiving the $400 each year. *Consequently, a combination of perceived rate of return and risk determines how much we'll pay now.*

Cap rates represent the percentage rate of return we'll require, expressed by their inverse ratios, as whole numbers. If you think a 20 percent annual return is required, the cap factor is 5 (100 percent divided by 20 percent = 5). Similarly, a 10 percent annual return results in a cap factor of 10; a 33 1/3 percent annual return results in a cap factor of 3.3. Since a riskier investment will require a higher annual return, *the greater the risk, the lower the cap factor; the lower the cap factor, the less a business is worth.*

Revenue Ruling 68-609 brings us close to an acceptable formula for valuing a business, but it's flawed. For starters, it's terribly out of date, having been issued when interest rates were around 5 percent. Plugging in an 8 to 10 percent return for tangible assets (i.e., cap factors of 10 to 12) and 10 to 20 percent for goodwill (i.e., cap factors of 5 to 10) has a tendency to make any business look like a good investment. Today's businesses have to compete with yields on bonds, Treasury bills, and money market accounts far in excess of what they were in 1968. Revenue Ruling 68-609 has a tendency to *overvalue* most businesses.

Revenue Ruling 68-609 is also conceptually flawed. As we've seen, when you buy a business you're not paying for the return that tangible assets can bring you but for the excess earnings they could bring if sold for cash and the cash invested.

Revenue Ruling 68-609 brings us close to a workable formula for valuing a business. We can get closer.

3. *A Modified (and Improved) Valuation Formula.* There're certain things we've learned about the balance sheet. We've seen that the balance sheet doesn't measure the value of assets, only what was *paid* for them. As for depreciable assets, it doesn't even do that, since the adjusted book value of these assets is net of depreciation. (Take a look at the balance sheet on page 32 to refresh your memory.) In recent years allowances for accelerated depreciation have driven the book values of depreciable assets down very fast and very far, so that book values have little relation to market values. In addition, in 1986 Congress changed the tax law to lessen the

depreciation allowed in any year on most assets. The result is that you probably won't be permitted to depreciate the assets you buy as rapidly as your seller did.

We've also seen that the income statement doesn't really reflect the true income of the business. Net income (the bottom line) is computed after the owner's salary has been taken. It also includes such bookkeeping entries as depreciation, which have no direct impact on cash. Do you want to buy a business based on what the balance sheet *says* the net worth of the business is or what is really is? Are you interested in a business's ability to generate ''accounting'' net income or real income?

Our modified formula takes off where the IRS's formula leaves off. It measures the real value of assets and the real income of the business. First we'll go through the formula; then we'll apply it.

Step 1: Value the assets and liabilities. Go through every item on the balance sheet and place a value on it. You won't have any problem valuing cash. If any of the accounts receivable are more than ninety days old, reduce them by a percentage, say 20 percent. Reduce any receivables older than sixty days by a lower percentage, say 10 percent. You might consider placing no value at all on receivables older than six months.

Do the same for inventory. You should discount it. There's a big difference between the cost of inventory before its sold and the price you can sell it for. Value the inventory at a figure no higher than what it cost to produce. Inventory that has been sitting on the shelf for more than six months should not be counted.

The fixed assets may be the most difficult group of assets to value. They may be worth far less or more (especially in the case of real estate) than the book values assigned to them.

Do the same for the liabilities. This should be easier, since liabilities have a tendency to remain fixed. If the business disputes a certain payable, take this into account; you may not have to pay it.

After you've valued the assets and the liabilities, subtract the liabilities from the assets. The result is the *adjusted net worth* of the business; what the net assets are really worth.

Step 2: Determine the earnings capacity of the adjusted net worth. In this step we're computing what the net assets could earn if they weren't used in business. To do this, you need to assume an average rate of return. In 1968 the IRS suggested using 8 to 10 percent. This is too low; try using 12 percent. Multiply the average rate of return (12 percent) by the adjusted rate of return. The result is the average earnings capacity for the adjusted net worth.

Step 3: Determine the adjusted pretax profits. Take the Net Profit (before taxes) entry shown on the income statement *adding back* such items as owner's salary and bonuses and such noncash expenses as depreciation and amortization costs. The result is the adjusted pretax profits.

Step 4: Determine excess earnings. Subtract the result in step 2 from the result in step 3. What you just did is subtract the earnings the tangible assets are capable of from the total real earnings of the business. You've arrived at the real value of goodwill for the year.

Step 5: Multiply the result in step 4 by a cap factor. You're now at the very heart of the problem. What kind of cap factor will you apply? At this point you're on your own. The full investigation you, your attorney, and accountant have conducted should give you a good idea whether a higher or lower cap rate is justified. Here's a hint: Considering that all businesses today have to compete with interest rates which recently have been very high, it's a rare privately held business that commands a cap factor in excess of 5. A cap factor of 5 means that an owner will settle for an annual return on investment of only 20 percent. This isn't too much of a premium above what someone could get from a high-yielding bond. It means that the business has been producing a steady stream of profits for a long time. It also means that profit will probably not be affected by a change in ownership. Many businesses sell at cap factors in the 2 to 3 range.

At the other end of the scale, many service businesses that rely heavily on the personalities, contacts and expertise of their owners can't command cap factors much in excess of 1. They're considered inherently too fraught with risk; a buyer has no way of knowing whether the success of the departing entreprenuer can be transferred.

Here's some help in determining the appropriate cap rate. Since it's a closely held business you're buying, the cap rate will be between 1 and 5. Let's *rate* the business as follows:

Risk	Extreme risk	1 2 ③ 4 5	Low risk
Competition	Very competitive	1 ② 3 4 5	Monopoly
Growth	Declining	1 2 3 ④ 5	Steady; annual
Industry	Declining industry	1 2 3 4 ⑤	Growing
Intangibles	Unappealing business	1 2 3 ④ 5	Highly appealing

3.5

Rate the target business on each of the above factors and take an average. The average is the cap factor.

Step 6: Add the result from step 5 to the adjusted net worth determined in step 1. The result is the total value of the business.

If at this point you're a little disappointed, you've a right to be. The formula required you to value the assets and liabilities, plug in an assumed rate of return for tangibles, and, worst of all, assume a cap rate. It's rather like being invited to dine at a fancy restaurant and being told that you'll be doing the cooking.

Let's apply the formula, making some assumptions. We know from the financial statements on pages 32 and 33 what Houston Sash & Door's book value and net pretax profits are. Let's make some assumptions regarding the adjusted values as follows:

Financial Statements (1985)		As Adjusted	
Net worth	$691,415	Adjusted net worth	$800,000
Earnings before		Adjusted earnings before	
taxes	$362,017	taxes	$440,982

The formula is applied as follows:

Step 2: $800,000 × .12 = $96,000 (earnings capacity of adjusted net worth)

Step 4: $440,982 − $96,000 = $344,982 (excess earnings)

Step 5: (Applying a cap factor of 3):

$344,982 × 3 = $1,034,946 (capitalized excess earnings)

Step 6: $1,034,946 capitalized excess earnings

<u>+ 800,000</u> adjusted net worth

<u>$1,834,946</u> total value of the business!

Is Houston Sash & Door worth $1,834,946? Hard to say. We plugged in a cap factor of 3. If you think a cap factor of 2 is fairer, the business is worth only $1,489,964. An appraiser may tell you Houston Sash & Door is worth $1,834,946. Is it? It is only if a buyer will pay it and the seller will take it. *A business is worth what a willing buyer will pay to a willing seller!*

WHEN TO PAY

Let's assume that you think Houston Sash & Door is really worth $1,800,000 and Mr. Houston is willing to part with it for this sum. Are you going to write a check for $1,800,000? I hope not!

If you don't have $1,800,000 handy, you have two choices. You can either borrow the money from a bank and write Mr. Houston a check for $1,800,000 or borrow the money from the seller, by having the seller carry you for all or part of the purchase price. Either way, buying the business will cost more than $1,800,000, since you'll have to pay interest to either the bank or Mr. Houston. In the case of a bank, you'll also have to pay loan origination fees, "points," and a host of other charges which result from the pleasure of doing business with a bank. Does it matter to whom you owe the money?

You bet it does. Let's assume that a month after the sale, you discover some disturbing things. You learn that Mr. Houston wasn't quite truthful with you when you spoke to him and when he signed the purchase agreement. There's a lawsuit against Houston Sash & Door you weren't told of. A supplier turns up with an outstanding bill that didn't appear on the financial statements. In fact, Mr. Houston's lack of candor might have been so great that had you known all the things he didn't tell you, you

wouldn't have bought the business. If you've already paid Mr.
Houston in full, your choices are limited to licking your wounds or
suing to get your money back. If you haven't already paid in full,
a wonderful option appears: You can write the seller informing
him of his misdeeds and notifying him you intend to retain part of
the purchase price pending resolution of all of the problem items.
At this point the seller is faced with the unpleasant options of waiv-
ing his rights to the withheld amount or suing to get the money
back. Lawsuits are expensive and bothersome. It's better to make
the seller decide whether to start a lawsuit to get his money than
for you to have to sue to get your money back.

Most businesses are sold by means of some form of seller carry.
A seller who wants all his money up front either has something to
hide or isn't interested in selling. Negotiating a seller carry will
ultimately cost you more, both in terms of a higher purchase price
and the interest costs. Nevertheless, you're in a more secure position than if you pay all or the majority of the price in cash.

NEGOTIATING THE SECURITY INTEREST

If you're like most buyers, you'll wind up being able to buy on
some form of seller carry. Whatever the amount and terms of the
promissory note you'll be required to sign, the seller will require
you to provide security for the payment of the note. It's only fair.
You wouldn't sell your house to anyone on a promissory note
unless you knew in advance that if the buyer didn't make the
required payments, you could get the house back. Moreover, having made the loan based on the buyer's credit, you wouldn't want
the buyer to be able to sell the house unless you were paid, or at
least not before your permission was obtained. The seller of
a business has the same concerns and is entitled to the same
security.

But don't give the seller too much security. Very often a seller
will demand a security interest in anything and everything. In
addition to a mortgage on the real estate and the fixed assets, the
seller may demand a security interest in your accounts receivable,
including the receivables you generate after the sale. The seller

may even ask for a security interest in any patent rights that have been sold or are generated after the sale.

You may think that as long as you keep paying on the promissory note there's no problem in granting a blanket security interest. Not exactly. At some point you may wish to expand your business, and you may well need to borrow money to do it. At this point, a bank will likely require that you provide security for *their* loan. If you've already granted a security interest in all your assets to the seller, the chances of the bank lending you any money will drop from good to slim.

If the seller insists on a blanket security interest, there's a possible middle ground you could try to negotiate. The seller may be willing to *subordinate* his security interest in favor of a lender who lends money for legitimate business reasons. Being subordinated means that the seller still will have a security interest, but the seller's security will be secondary (to use bankers' lingo: *junior*) to the bank's. You won't be able to borrow money secured by business assets to take a European vacation, but you will be able to borrow for valid business purposes.

CREATIVE BUYING (I): THE BOOTSTRAP ACQUISITION

Take another quick look at Houston Sash & Door's balance sheet (page 32). The business has lots of cash, more than may be required to conduct operations. If you're looking at a business heavy in cash, an opportunity may exist to use the business's own assets to finance the acquisition: the bootstrap acquisition.

A bootstrap acquisition will work only if the business being sold is incorporated and only if you're planning to buy the stock of the business, rather than the assets. As we'll see in Chapter 6, there're plenty of good reasons *not* to buy the stock and to insist on an asset purchase. But if you can arrange a bootstrap acquisition, a stock purchase may be in order.

Bootstrap acquisitions work like this: If you can't afford to buy all the seller's stock, buy part of it and on the same day—*at the same moment!*—have the *business* buy the seller's remaining stock. The business then retires the stock it bought from the seller. When this happens, you wind up with all the *issued and outstanding* stock of the business, just as if you had bought it all directly from the seller. You wind up with a business with a lower net worth than it otherwise would have (since you've depleted the cash asset) but you've used someone else's money (the business itself) to finance the sale.

Let's take a quick example: Seller owns 100 percent of the stock of ABC, Inc. Buyer and Seller agree that $1,000,000 is a fair price for the business. Seller wants $400,000 down, which Buyer doesn't have, but which ABC does. The parties agree that Seller will sell 40 percent of his stock to ABC for $400,000. Seller will simultaneously sell 60 percent of his stock to Buyer for a $600,000 promissory note, as follows:

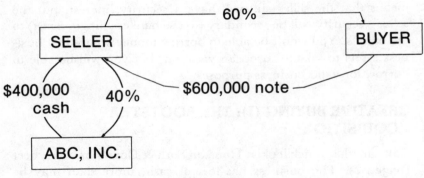

Figure 5.1.

Had Buyer bought all of Seller's stock, Buyer would, of course, have owned 100 percent of the stock. But after ABC, Inc. retires the 40 percent it bought from Seller, Buyer's 60 percent *becomes* 100 percent of the issued and outstanding stock. Buyer gains the same 100 percent ownership without having to take $400,000 out of pocket.

The IRS doesn't have any problem with the bootstrap acquisition. In fact, the IRS already has given the technique its seal of approval by issuing a favorable revenue ruling. But here's what the IRS won't permit: If you go a step further and have the corporation make the payments on the promissory note you owe to the seller, the IRS will assert that the payments represent an indirect *dividend* the corporation paid to you so you could pay the seller. This is the worst place to wind up because corporate dividends are income to you but they're not deductible to the corporation. The best way to handle the payments to the seller is to have the corporation make salary payments to you to cover the payments. The salary will be taxable to you, but unlike dividends, salary *is* deductible to the corporation.

CREATIVE BUYING (II): THE EARNOUT

Perhaps you can't agree on a purchase price with the seller. Perhaps you don't want to agree. You may find that no matter how carefully you've analyzed the business, there's some aspect of it that leaves you uneasy. You may feel that the continuing purchases of a major customer is questionable. You may be uncertain about whether a key employee will stay on. In short, you don't feel that past performance is a sure indicator of future earnings. For whatever reason, you can't nail down a price.

All may not be lost. The seller may be willing to sell the business on an earnout basis. Under an earnout, the purchase price of the business isn't fixed at the closing. Instead, the *final purchase price is determined by future events*. Negotiating an earnout requires the seller to have confidence you'll succeed in business after you buy. It usually requires intense negotiations.

Here's an example of how it works. Let's say that the seller wants $1,000,000 for the business. For whatever reason, you're not willing to pay more than $700,000. You feel that present earnings will support a $700,000 purchase price, but there are so many unknowns and problems in this business that you're not sure you'll be able to increase earnings sufficient to warrant a $1,000,000 price. You offer the seller the following: "Mr. Seller, I'll pay you $700,000 on terms we still need to negotiate. The business has annual sales of $300,000. If in the year after I buy sales go to $400,000, you get X percent of the increase. If in the year after that sales go to $500,000, you get X percent from

$300,000 to $400,000 and Y percent from $400,000 to $500,000. In the third year you get Z percent in excess of $500,000." Of course, the fierce negotiating results when buyer and seller try to replace X, Y, and Z with numbers.

If you agree to this earnout formula and sales don't increase much past $300,000 (or decline!), you wind up paying no more than $700,000. But depending on what X, Y, and Z are, if sales increase substantially, you may wind up paying, and the seller may wind up receiving, far more than the $1,000,000 the seller would have been happy with. Each of you is betting on the future.

An earnout formula has a way of accomplishing a few things a fixed sales price won't. To begin with, it makes the seller put his money where his mouth is. Most sellers try to convince buyers how much opportunity there is for growth in their business. By offering an earnout you are in effect saying: "Mr. Seller, I really believe you when you tell me how fast this business can grow. But if *you* believe what you're saying, you shouldn't have any problem in agreeing to *share* in that growth with me!"

An earnout also has the delightful side effect of having the seller really interested in your success after you buy. If you're successful in negotiating a consulting agreement with the seller, an earnout will give the seller a real incentive to consult, rather than merely show up. The seller will be motivated to ensure that good relations with customers and suppliers are maintained; the seller's income is dependent on it.

You may have noticed in our example that we based the earnout formula on sales rather than profits. It takes a really dumb seller to agree to an earnout based on profits. The owner of a business has too many opportunities to deflate or eliminate profits, even if sales are increasing. An owner will have no problem buying new machinery, increasing inventory, hiking salaries, or doing a thousand other things that will have the effect of eliminating the seller's earnout while improving the business. You're not likely to negotiate an earnout based on profits.

You can use an earnout formula in addition to any other terms or creative financing mechanism; it's not merely a substitute. For example, it can be used in conjunction with a bootstrap acquisi-

CREATIVE BUYING(II): THE EARNOUT **87**

tion. Go back to the example we used when we discussed bootstrap acquisitions. Part of the purchase price was to have been paid by the buyer with a $600,000 promissory note. The terms of the note can be left open, subject to an earnout formula. By doing this, you have the best of two worlds: The business buys part of the seller's stock, and the seller has a continuing interest in the success of the business.

Chapter **6**

NEGOTIATING THE SALE (II): STOCK PURCHASES AND ASSET PURCHASES

Equally important to determining how much and when you're going to pay for the business is determining just what it is you're going to buy. In fact, the resolution of this issue with your seller will (or at least *should*) have a bearing on the price you'll be willing to pay. Consequently, negotiations as to what you're going to buy should precede, or at least be concurrent with, your price and terms negotiations.

If the seller conducts his or her business as a sole proprietorship or partnership (more on that in Chapter 9), you have no choice; all you can buy is the seller's assets. If the seller conducts his business as a corporation, however, and if the corporation owns the business's assets, there're two possible ways to buy the business. You can buy the assets *from* the business (a straight asset purchase) or you can obtain the assets by buying the business itself, by buying the corporate stock from the corporation's owners, its shareholders.

At first blush, it may seem there's little difference between these two methods. But, as we'll soon see, there's all the difference in the world. *For some very significant reasons, the seller usually will prefer to sell the stock, and the buyer usually will prefer to buy the assets.* As a result, if both buyer and seller know what they're doing, the negotiations on this issue can be ferocious. On occasion a seller will simply say

"No sale unless you buy the stock." At other times, a buyer will say "All I'm interested in buying are the assets." Sometimes the issue is resolved by the seller selling the stock but the buyer paying less, or the buyer taking the assets and paying more.

Before we get into the ways in which buyer and seller are helped and harmed by each method, let's take a quick look at what each method entails. Let's assume that XYZ Corporation has two owners, Messrs. Jones and Smith, with Jones owning 90 percent of the stock and Smith owning 10 percent. XYZ buys flowers and distributes them to retail florists. It has everything you'd expect this type of business to have: an inventory of flowers, some furniture and equipment, supply contracts with and accounts receivable from its customers (the retail florists), and accounts payable to its suppliers. XYZ also still owes on the notes it signed to buy some equipment and has a lease on its warehouse and corporate offices. Ms. Green wants to buy the business and thinks she wants to pay approximately $100,000, to be paid $50,000 in cash and $50,000 by means of a promissory note.

If Ms. Green buys the stock, the purchase goes like this:

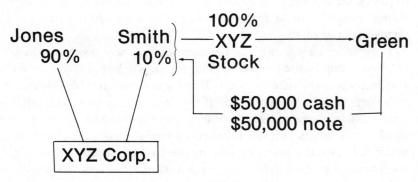

Figure 6.1.

As you can see, the transaction is relatively simple: Messrs. Jones and Smith merely exchange their stock for cash and a promissory note. XYZ Corporation isn't even a party to the deal. Nothing happens to the assets, accounts payable and receivable, leases, and contracts of XYZ.

Now let's see what happens if Ms. Green buys the assets of
XYZ. In buying the assets, she'll also be required to take the payables, as follows:

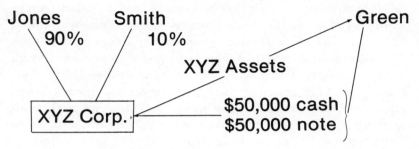

Figure 6.2.

Ms. Green now owns everything that XYZ owned. Messrs. Jones
and Smith, who weren't parties to this transaction, still own all the
stock of XYZ, but now XYZ has only two assets, $50,000 in cash
and a $50,000 note.

It still may look as though Ms. Green arrives at roughly the
same destination, regardless of the route she takes to get there.
Now let's examine closely the differences to Jones, Smith, and
Green between a stock sale and an asset sale.

HIDDEN LIABILITIES

On the morning after the sale one of XYZ's customers, a local
florist, sues XYZ, claiming that a late delivery of a large shipment
of flowers severely harmed its business, since the flowers arrived
after Mother's Day, not before as required by the purchase contract. It appears that the negligence of one of XYZ's warehouse
employees (who shipped the goods to Columbus, Georgia instead
of Columbus, Ohio) caused the delay, and XYZ is going to have
to pay. But who owns XYZ? If Ms. Green bought only the assets,
she doesn't own XYZ; Jones and Smith still do. XYZ will probably have to pay the judgment to the florist out of the $50,000 it's
received from the sale of the assets. But if Ms. Green bought Jones

and Smith's stock, she owns XYZ, and the judgment will have to be paid from *her* business. Big difference!

The problem of unknown, or *contingent,* liabilities is one of the major reasons sellers want to sell their stock and buyers often refuse to buy the stock, preferring to buy the assets. Sellers want to know that after they sell their business, they're done with it and they won't have to worry about any problems coming out of the woodwork after they sell. Buyers want just the opposite. Buyers want the assurance that what they see is what they get, period. Having carefully reviewed the balance sheet and income statement of the business and having arrived at a purchase price based on this review, buyers don't want some liability of the business they bought to pop out and zap them.

Let's assume that no matter how tough Ms. Green is in her negotiations, Messrs. Jones and Smith simply won't sell anything but their stock; they're just not interested in an asset sale. Is there anything Ms. Green can do to avoid (or at least mitigate) the problem of hidden liabilities? There is, but it's a weak substitute for buying the assets. Ms. Green might be successful in getting an *indemnification clause* written into the purchase agreement, in which Jones and Smith agree that (1) "there are no hidden liabilities we know of" and (2) if any liabilities pop up caused by us before we sold the business, we'll pay them." Even if an indemnification clause can be extracted from the seller, it's a weak substitute, since it doesn't prevent the local florist from suing XYZ Corporation and collecting a judgment from it. It just means that after the florist has collected the judgment, XYZ Corporation will be able to turn around and sue Jones and Smith for the money it's paid. But what if Jones and Smith don't have the money to pay or have retired to New Zealand and can't even be found, much less sued? An indemnification clause can be strengthened by structuring the sale so that if XYZ has to pay on a hidden liability, the amount paid is deducted from any amount that still remains to be paid on the promissory note. That's better but still might not do the job. The promissory note may have already been paid once the liability arises or may be for an amount far in excess of the note. In this case, the buyer of corporate stock is still stuck.

By this time it should be obvious to you that, as a buyer, you must do everything you can to ferret out any problems lurking in the seller's business before you close the sale. You should be even more diligent if you are, for whatever reason (and there may be some good reasons, which we'll get to later), going to buy the stock.

KNOWN ASSETS AND LIABILITIES

One of the big advantages to a buyer in an asset purchase is that since only the *parts* of the business, rather than the whole, are being purchased, the buyer may, with some tough negotiating, pick and choose which assets he or she will buy and which liabilities will be assumed. Ms. Green may say to the sellers: "See that truck over there? I'm planning on buying a new truck, and I won't need yours. You keep it, and you can keep paying on the debt that remains to be paid on the truck." The purchase price of the business (i.e., all the assets) may be lower (or *higher* if the debt on the truck is greater than its value), and Ms. Green winds up buying only what she wants.

There are, however, certain liabilities a buyer may not be able to avoid, even if he doesn't want them and even if the sale is structured as an asset sale. Here's a rundown.

The Bulk Sales Act

Every state has a law dealing with bulk transfers, usually referred to by lawyers, accountants, and brokers as the bulk sales act. It comes into play only if the sale is an asset sale, since, as we've seen, if the stock is sold there's no effect on the assets or liabilities of the business. Bulk sales acts are designed to give some protection to the creditors of a business whose assets are being sold and whose liabilities are being transferred. Properly used, the state bulk sales act will protect the buyer.

Here's how it works. If the assets of a business are to be sold and that business has *inventory*, the buyer and seller must comply with the provisions of the bulk sales act *before* the business is sold. If the act isn't complied with, the creditors of the business can sue the *buyer* to collect their debts, even if the buyer didn't agree in the purchase agreement to assume the debts. In most states the bulk sales act applies only if the business being sold has inventory. In these states, if you're buying a service business, such as a restaurant or a barber shop, you needn't worry about complying. The seller will remain liable for the debts unless you've agreed in the purchase contract to pay them. In some states the bulk sales act applies with respect to the sale of any business.

The buyer and seller comply with the bulk sales act as follows: First, the seller provides the buyer with a sworn affidavit that lists the names and addresses of all the seller's business creditors and states the amount of each debt. Even if the seller disputes the debt or isn't sure if it's owed, the debt must be listed. Then the buyer must send each creditor a notice, at least ten days prior to the sale, stating that the transfer of the assets is about to take place. Depending on the law of the state in which the sale is taking place, the buyer may have to either state that he will pay each debt at the closing or, more likely, promise to pay each debt as it comes due. If the seller fails to list any business creditors on the affidavit, the seller remains liable for it, not the buyer.

As you can see, the bulk sales act works to protect only the buyer, not the seller. If both parties ignore the law, the sale can go through, but the seller's creditors will be able to go against the buyer to collect their debts. Because of this, sellers often attempt to convince buyers to skip complying with the law, arguing that it's an unnecessary hassle. More often, sellers will offer their own indemnification of liabilities as a substitute. But the indemnfication here is the same weak substitute as it is in the case of hidden liabilities. If the seller doesn't have the money to pay or can't be found, the buyer is stuck.

Even if you're planning to assume all the liabilities of the seller's business, you still should comply with the bulk sales act. The seller may have "forgotten" about a liability. For example, Messrs. Jones and Smith may have known they were about to be sued or may have already been sued and merely "forgotten" to tell Ms. Green. Comply with the law; you'll be better off.

Pension and Profit-Sharing Plan Liabilities

The seller may have instituted a *qualified* pension plan or profit-sharing plan for the employees. A qualified plan is one established and operated under the Employee Retirement Income Security Act of 1974 (ERISA). Under an ERISA plan, particularly a pension plan, the employer is required to make annual contributions to the plan, to ensure that sufficient funds are available to pay employees' pension benefits or meet their share of the profit-sharing plan. But your seller may be behind in the payments or not be sure what future payments will be needed to comply with the plan's requirements. If you find that your seller does have one of these plans, you *must* get your attorney (or, even better, an attorney familiar with the operations of these plans) to check to see what is the plan's funding status.

Labor Law Liabilities

If any of your seller's employees are members of a union, you must be very careful. If the sale is structured as a stock sale, nothing will change; your relations with the union will be exactly the same as before the sale. Only the stock will have changed hands; the corporation remains unaffected. You may be surprised to learn, however, that if your seller's employees have entered into a collective bargaining agreement with a union and you buy only the assets, you'll not be required to comply with the terms of the agreement. The collective bargaining agreement is treated like any other contract your seller entered into which you didn't assume. Of course, if you plan to retain most or all of the seller's employees, as a practical matter you won't be able to disavow the terms of the agreement if you want them to continue working. But if you don't plan to keep them, buying only the assets will free you from the terms your seller negotiated with the union. The only exception to this is a situation where the National Labor Relations Board (NLRB) determines that the sale of assets is a sham accomplished for the purpose of walking away from a labor agreement. In a true arm's-length sale of a business, this shouldn't be a problem at all.

There're certain labor law responsibilities you may not be able to avoid even if you buy the assets. If the selling corporation was found by the NLRB to have committed an unfair labor practice, either by firing people who were attempting to organize the employees or by a host of other prohibited activities, whatever liabilities (including back pay awards to employees) result from such a determination are going to follow you if you knew about the practices and didn't stop them. Also, if the NLRB required your seller to *recognize* the union as the legitimate representative of the employees and ordered your seller to bargain in good faith with the union, these obligations will follow you, even if you buy only the assets.

The learning in all this is that you must dig as deep as you can before buying, no matter how you buy. But your risks are greater if you buy the stock, for all these lurking liabilities and responsibilities will surely follow you if you buy the stock.

TAX BENEFITS AND PITFALLS

Unless you're an accountant or a tax lawyer, you probably view the subject of taxes with much of the same fear and loathing as you view a trip to the dentist. All too often buyers and sellers of businesses (*and their lawyers!*) go about their merry way, thinking "we'll let the accountants worry about the taxes." That's crazy. After the buyer and seller have closed the deal, there's very little the accountants can do about taxes except set up the books and live with the deal that's been given them.

How important are the tax effects of the way you structure the sale? Let's go back to Messrs. Jones and Smith selling the flower business to Ms. Green. She was willing, based on her evaluation of XYZ Corporation's assets and earnings, to pay $100,000 for the business. But what if the sale was structured so poorly as to taxes for Messrs. Jones and Smith that they won't receive $100,000 but only $80,000, or so poorly for Ms. Green that she won't wind up paying $100,000 but $120,000? Big difference!

Before examining the tax effects of stock sales and asset sales to buyer and seller, let's review a little recent history.

On October 22, 1986, President Reagan signed the Tax Reform Act of 1986. The Act constituted the most sweeping change in tax law in a generation. For our purposes, here are the most significant changes:

- The highest rate of tax on individual taxpayers was reduced from 50 to 28 percent. The former eleven tax brackets were replaced by two brackets, 15 and 28 percent.
- The capital gains deduction was eliminated. Before its repeal the highest rate of tax on long-term capital gains (for taxpayers in the former highest bracket of 50 percent) was 20 percent. As a result of this change, there's now no difference between the tax on capital gains and ordinary income.
- The investment tax credit was eliminated. A person who bought business equipment used to qualify for a tax credit equal to 10 percent of the purchase price of most new equipment. The investment tax credit for used equipment was also repealed.
- Under the old law, corporations that sold assets didn't have to pay any taxes on the sale. After the Tax Reform Act many, but not all, sales of assets will be subject to tax. This is the most complex area of all, since for sales of assets totalling under $5,000,000, the rules don't all go into effect until January 1, *1989*. More on that later.

All this has a profound effect on how buyers and sellers will want to structure the sale of a business. Let's examine closely the differences between asset sales and stock sales to the buyer and the seller.

1. *Asset Sales Viewed by the Seller.* Let's assume that Messrs. Jones and Smith and Ms. Green agree that XYZ's assets and liabilities have the following values:

Assets		Liabilities	
Inventory on Hand	$10,000	Accounts Payable	$3,000
Furniture and Fixtures	6,000		
Accounts Receivable	19,000		

The net assets have a $32,000 value ($35,000 – $3,000 = $32,000). If Ms. Green pays $100,000 for the business, the difference between what she pays and the value of the tangible assets represents her payment for goodwill, what she feels the assets can earn.

But let's look at Furniture and Fixtures more carefully. Let's assume that although they're worth $6,000, on the XYZ balance sheet the entry under Furniture and Fixtures is only $700. The reason is that XYZ took depreciation deductions on the furniture and fixtures, which reduced XYZ's tax basis in these items to $700. When XYZ sells these assets for an agreed-upon price of $6,000, XYZ's *gain* of $5,300 ($6,000 – $700 = $5,300) is subject to tax. Before the Tax Reform Act of 1986 the sale of these assets might have qualified for preferential capital gains treatment; they don't anymore. They're subject to the corporation's normal tax rates. The same holds true of the inventory. If the sales price exceeds the tax basis, the difference is subject to tax.

But the worst is yet to come. Let's assume that XYZ sells its assets for $50,000 in cash and a $50,000 promissory note. Let's also assume that when Jones and Smith formed XYZ they did so with very little invested cash. Let's assume they each invested $1,000, which is not at all unusual. If and when XYZ distributes the $50,000 in cash and the $50,000 promissory note to Jones and Smith, they'll have to pay *another* tax, calculated on the difference between the $100,000 they receive and the $2,000 initial investment, that is, a tax on their $98,000 gain! Before the Tax Reform Act Jones and Smith qualified for the capital gains deductions, which means that the tax on the $98,000 gain couldn't exceed 20 percent. Now the gain will be taxed at 28 percent.

There's a little light in the darkness. If the sale occurs before January 1, 1989, and is for a price under $5,000,000, XYZ might avoid the tax on the sale of *some* of its assets. More on that a little later.

2. *Stock Sales Viewed by the Seller.* Take another look at Figure 6.1 (page 90). When Jones and Smith sell their stock to Ms. Green, Ms. Green will pay Jones and Smith directly; XYZ is not a party

to the sale. Jones and Smith will pay the same tax on the gain from the receipt of the $100,000 from Ms. Green as they would have paid had XYZ sold the assets and then distributed the proceeds to them: $100,000 – $2,000 = $98,000 gain. The difference, of course, is that by directly selling their stock they've avoided the tax XYZ would have paid had XYZ sold its assets to Ms. Green.

Do sellers prefer to sell their stock or have their corporations sell the assets? Obviously, sellers prefer direct stock sales. In addition to the nontax advantages to a seller, selling the stock avoids a lot of taxes.

Bear one thing in mind. The *seller* usually will be subject to taxes on the sale. Whatever tax advantages or disadvantages arise from the manner in which the sale is structured will help or hurt the buyer down the road.

3. *Stock Sales Viewed by the Buyer.* Let's go back to the $6,000 in furniture and fixtures that XYZ depreciated down to $700. If Jones and Smith sell their stock to Ms. Green (which, as we've seen, is a transaction that doesn't involve XYZ) nothing has happened to the furniture and fixtures. *They* haven't been sold. This means that Ms. Green must continue depreciating the furniture and fixtures in the same manner that Jones and Smith did, which in this case means there are only $700 in depreciation deductions left. If XYZ had paid $6,000 for furniture and fixtures, it would have qualified for $6,000 in depreciation deductions. The effect of Ms. Green buying Jones and Smith's stock directly is to lose $5,300 in depreciation deductions—this in addition to all the non-tax disadvantages to the buyer we've already discussed.

4. *Asset Sales Viewed by the Buyer.* We've pretty much answered this one. If Ms. Green (or a corporation formed by Ms. Green) buys the assets, Ms. Green will qualify for a new round of depreciation on those assets that qualify for depreciation, based on what she paid for them. If she paid $6,000 for furniture and fixtures, she'll qualify for $6,000 worth of depreciation deductions.

As you can see, there's really no sound tax reason for a seller to want to sell the assets (assuming there's any potential for gain

inherent in the assets) and no good tax reason for a buyer to want
to buy the stock.

A SUGGESTED COMPROMISE: ASSET SALES AND THE "12-MONTH LIQUIDATION"

There's no getting around the fact that smart sellers will always
want to sell their stock. But let's assume that you can convince the
seller to sell the assets. There's a way to mitigate, and perhaps
even eliminate, the harsher tax effects of an asset sale to a seller.

In 1954 Congress realized that hitting sellers for two taxes on
one sale was somewhat unfair and enacted Section 337 of the tax
code, the "12-month liquidation." Section 337 provided that if a
corporate seller sells the assets and then distributes the proceeds of
the sale within twelve months, there would be a tax to the shareholders when they receive the proceeds but no tax to the corporation on the sale. In our example, this means that when XYZ sells
the assets to Ms. Green, there would be no tax on the sale to Ms.
Green but Jones and Smith would pay the tax on the difference
between the $100,000 they receive and their $2,000 investment in
the corporation.

The problem is that the Tax Reform Act repealed most of Section 337! Here's what's left: If a corporation sells its assets before
January 1, 1989, for less than $5,000,000, the assets that used to
qualify for capital gains treatment (buildings, plant, equipment,
furniture and fixtures, etc.) can still be sold tax free if the corporation liquidates the proceeds to the shareholders within twelve
months. The assets that never qualified for capital gains treatment, such as inventory or accounts receivable, are subject to tax
on the sale, with the proceeds subject to tax when distributed. In
other words, inventory and accounts receivable are now subject to
double taxation. What's worse, the sale of *all* assets will be subject
to double tax starting on January 1, 1989.

Sellers now need to be cagey. If a seller can allocate most of the
sales price to capital assets, away from ordinary assets such as
inventory, the seller can avoid paying two taxes. In our example,
this means allocating more of the purchase price toward the furni-

ture and fixtures and less in the direction of inventory and accounts receivable. As a buyer you shouldn't mind, since the more you pay for depreciable assets such as furniture and fixtures, the more depreciation you qualify for. But be careful: You don't want to allocate too little of the purchase price toward inventory to customers for $12,000; you'll pay income tax on the $8,000 profit. If you allocate $10,000 toward the inventory (what we originally thought the inventory was worth), the taxable profit will be only $2,000.

The bottom line here is that if the result of the negotiations is an asset sale, you and your seller need to be careful to draft the purchase agreement so that it specifies how the purchase price will be allocated among the various assets. This a good place to involve your accountant.

CONGRESS CLOSES A LOOPHOLE

In situations where the assets (as opposed to the stock) of a business were sold, buyers and sellers had a nifty way of ganging up on the tax collectors. Even though buyers and sellers could (and should) allocate the total purchase price among the various assets, there wasn't a requirement that they must, and if they did, no requirement that buyers and sellers allocate consistently. The result was that a buyer would allocate the purchase price among the assets in a manner resulting in favorable tax treatment to him and the seller would allocate differently if it resulted in favorable tax treatment to him. The IRS, without the resources or ability to value the assets or compare the buyer's and the seller's tax returns, was left holding the bag.

The most common allocation was one in which a high value was placed on the depreciable assets and a low or no value was placed on the goodwill. Since goodwill can't be depreciated or amortized, buyers always opted for the lowest possible allocation to goodwill. If the purchase agreement was silent as to the allocation among assets, buyers often wouldn't allocate to goodwill at all, choosing instead to allocate the purchase price to those assets that could produce the largest deductions. Buyers would do this by inflating the purchase price of depreciable assets. For example, if a machine was worth $50,000, the buyer would allocate $100,000 of the overall purchase price to the machine. The $100,000 amount would represent the buyer's tax basis in the machine, and the buyer would obtain $100,000 in depreciation deductions over the next five years.

The Tax Reform Act of 1986 changed all that. Buyers and sellers now must allocate among the assets. Worse, they must do so in a manner favorable to the IRS! Under current law, the total purchase price of the assets of a business must be allocated in the following order: first, to cash; second, to marketable securities such as readily tradeable stocks and bonds; next, to all tangible and intangible assets at their current fair market values; last, to goodwill. The opportunity for hanky-panky has been eliminated, at least theoretically. No longer may a buyer allocate $100,000 of purchase price to a machine worth only $50,000. The result is that more of the purchase price must be allocated toward nondeductible goodwill.

The IRS hasn't yet issued all the rules. But you can bet that when issued, buyers and sellers both will be required to report their allocations to the IRS and those allocations will have to be consistent.

Is the loophole closed entirely? Not really. The new rules place a premium on buyers and sellers allocating *away from the sale of assets in their entirety* in favor of such items as agreements not to compete and consulting agreements. Here's an example: A business whose tangible and intangible assets are worth $400,000 might sell for $1,000,000. Under the new rules, $600,000 must be allocated to goodwill, affording the buyer no deductions. If part of the $600,000 were allocated to a noncompetition agreement and/or a consulting agreement, the buyer would be able to deduct payments under these agreements as they're made. This type of allocation doesn't adversely affect the seller. With the elimination of the distinction between capital gains and ordinary income, the seller won't care whether money received is from the sale of goodwill or received under a noncompetition or consulting agreement.

REALLY CAGEY STRUCTURING: THE AGREEMENT NOT TO COMPETE

Let's assume that January 1, 1989, has come and gone. This means that no matter how buyer and seller allocate the purchase price among the assets, the seller will pay a tax on any gain obtained from the sales of appreciated assets. How the allocation is made may not matter to the seller. But the allocation could make a great deal of difference to you as a buyer.

Let's say that on January 2, 1989, Ms. Green says to Messrs. Jones and Smith: "Rather than pay you $100,000 for your business, I'll pay you $50,000 for the business and $50,000 for your agreement not to compete with XYZ for two years after the sale, payable over two years." Ms. Green is being very smart. She'll be able to amortize the $50,000 she pays for the agreement not to compete over the two-year term of the agreement, deducting $25,000 per year. This is a far faster write-off than she could obtain from any of the assets she buys, and infinitely faster than she could obtain from any allocation to land, inventory, or goodwill, which cannot be depreciated or amortized at all.

Consider an allocation of a part of the purchase price to an agreement not to compete any time you are fortunate enough to negotiate an asset sale. If the seller is insistent on selling only the stock, you still may be successful in allocating part of the purchase price to a covenant not to compete. Ms. Green could have said to Messrs. Jones and Smith: "All right, I'll buy the stock, but I'll pay only $50,000 for it. I'll pay another $50,000 for your agreement not to compete for two years." The tax effect to Jones and Smith is the same as if the stock was sold for $100,000 without an agreement not to compete. But it means all the difference in the world to Ms. Green. Had she bought the stock for $100,000, she couldn't depreciate or amortize anything, other than have XYZ continue to depreciate the assets in the same way it did before the sale. By allocating $50,000 to an agreement not to compete, she can amortize $50,000 over two years. (If Jones and Smith are smart, they'll say to Ms. Green: "We get no benefit from giving you an agreement not to compete, but you get a big tax break. If you want to allocate $50,000 to the agreement not to compete, we demand that the purchase price of the assets be increased from $50,000 to $55,000.'')

A buyer has to be very careful when structuring an allocation to an agreement not to compete. The IRS is not populated by dummies, and its agents know why allocations are made to noncompetition agreements. They also know they'll collect more taxes if they're successful in recharacterizing an agreement not to compete as nondeductible goodwill. The courts have not been uniform as to whether they'll uphold allocations to noncompetition agreements. What most courts look for is whether there's some ostensible business purpose for the agreement other than tax benefits. If everyone knew that the sellers were planning to move to New Zealand the day after the sale, with no possibility of competing with the buyer's business, the buyer will be skating on thin ice. The same is true if the agreement requires that payments continue even after the seller dies. In both cases, it's obvious the buyer wasn't really interested in buying the seller's agreement not to compete.

If you're successful in obtaining an allocation to an agreement not to compete, make sure that your (and your lawyer's) files reflect some hard bargaining concerning the agreement and that you and the seller didin't merely back out a part of the already agreed-upon total purchase price for the noncompetition agreement. This probably means you'll have to educate your seller as to the adverse tax effects of such an agreement to him or her, if your seller isn't very astute. The alternative can be a rather uncomfortable session with the IRS.

OTHER ADVANTAGES AND DISADVANTAGES

Are there any disadvantages to a buyer buying the assets or advantages in buying the stock? There are. One disadvantage to a buyer when the assets are bought is that it's most likely that state and local taxing authorities will require that a *sales tax* be paid, the same as when you buy personal assets in a store. To the extent the buyer is liable for state and local sales tax, it increases the cost of buying the business.

There're a few areas in which a stock purchase is preferable to an asset purchase. Here's a rundown:

Ease of Sale

One advantage that a stock purchase has over an asset purchase is that it's so much easier to accomplish. If Jones and Smith sell their stock in XYZ to Ms. Green, all they need do is endorse the certificates to Ms. Green by signing their names on the reverse side, and that's it. If XYZ sells its assets to Ms. Green, the sale becomes far more complex. Title to each asset must be changed, and the new title then recorded with the county. If XYZ chooses to effectuate the sale by means of a twelve-month liquidation (before January 1, 1989), it will have to adopt a plan of liquidation and liquidate XYZ within twelve months of the sale. Since a sale of assets represents the action of the corporation, rather than the individuals who own it, XYZ will have to conduct shareholders' and directors' meetings approving the sale.

This presents another problem with an asset sale. Let's assume that Mr. Smith, who owns 10 percent of the stock of XYZ, *doesn't want to sell the business.* If the sale is structured as a stock sale, Mr. Jones will sell his 90 percent interest in XYZ Corporation to Ms. Green, more than enough to give her all the control of XYZ she'll need. She may have a cantankerous minority shareholder on her hands, but this needn't cramp her style. On the other hand, if the sale is structured as an asset sale and Mr. Smith doesn't approve of the sale, most states grant Mr. Smith *appraisal rights* to have his stock appraised and bought from him. To this extent, Ms. Green will receive a somewhat smaller business and presumably pay somewhat less.

Retention of Corporate Rights

There're a few situations where the corporation owns a valuable right or asset essential to the conduct of business *that cannot be trans-*

ferred. In such a case, a buyer has no choice but to buy the stock of the business from its owners. A broadcast license owned by a radio station, a liquor license owned by a restaurant, a franchise granted to a corporation to manufacture a product or operate within a territory, a patent—all may be owned by the corporation. If these valuable assets can't be transferred, there's no choice but to buy the stock.

There's one valuable corporate asset that usually can be transferred in an asset sale: the corporation's *name.* If "XYZ Corporation" is known throughout the floral business and Ms. Green wants to continue using this name, she should be able to buy the right to use the name, as she would any other asset. If this is her intention, the purchase contract should specify that after the sale neither Jones nor Smith can use the name or any other name similar to it. This means that, after the sale of assets has been accomplished, Jones and Smith will have to change the name of their corporation. A buyer's desire to use the seller's business name (whether it's the corporation's actual name or a trade name used by the corporation) shouldn't require that the sale be structured as a sale of the stock.

Retention of Corporate Advantages

Similar to the retention of the corporation's nontransferable rights, there're certain advantages the corporation has that may be lost if the assets are purchased. For example, XYZ Corporation may have established a favorable liability insurance rating by having made few insurance claims in the past. If the assets are bought, the buyer might have to obtain new insurance without the favorable rating at a higher cost. Likewise, the seller's corporation may have developed a favorable unemployment compensation rating, again by having filed few claims in the past. Once again, that favorable rating may not be transferable in an asset purchase.

Rights under the Securities Laws

Let's assume that no matter diligent Ms. Green was in her investigation of the affairs of XYZ Corporation, Jones and Smith were successful in hiding a few skeletons from her. In fact, they simply lied to her, and many of the promises and representations they made to her when they signed the purchase agreement simply weren't true. Now Ms. Green finds that XYZ wasn't nearly as profitable as she was led to believe. Now she (and her lawyer) want to sue Jones and Smith for fraud. She can, but garden-variety common law fraud is more difficult to prove than securities fraud, that is, a fraud perpetrated in the sale of stock. If Ms. Green bought the assets, she can't sue for securities fraud, because she didn't buy any securities. Had she bought the stock from Jones and Smith, however, she would be able to sue under state and federal securities laws, and have an easier time getting her money back from Jones and Smith.

Are these advantages enough to overcome the substantial tax and liability advantages to a buyer that accrue from buying the assets? Probably not. After a careful investigation of all the facts, most buyers come to the conclusion that buying the assets, and letting the sellers keep their corporation, is exactly where they want to be.

Chapter 7

NEGOTIATING THE SALE (III): THE LOOK-SEE, CONSULTING AGREEMENTS, AND NONCOMPETITION AGREEMENTS

There're a few items remaining that need to be negotiated with your seller. Depending on your situation, these items may be equally or more important than the purchase price.

THE LOOK-SEE

Remember Tom Brown back in Chapter 1 who bought a record shop before he had the opportunity to experience how a record shop operated? Remember how surprised he was at how boring it was and how much he hated dealing with teenagers and their insane rock music? Wouldn't Tom Brown have avoided a terrible mistake if he'd been able to get a feel of what it's like to run a record shop before he bought it?

This is what a look-see is all about: being able to spend some time in the business before you're obligated to buy it. A look-see is vitally important simply because no amount of investigation can be as meaningful as spending some time in the trenches, while you learn firsthand what owning and operating the business will be like.

Getting a seller to agree to a look-see isn't easy. Many sellers simply won't consider it. They've some pretty good reasons for refusing.

A seller who has something to hide won't give you a look-see. But even those who don't have anything to hide have something to fear in allowing you to spend some time in the business before you're obligated to buy. A business dependent on any kind of trade secret, be it recipes for baking pies or the identity of certain suppliers, isn't going to be thrilled at the prospect of a stranger poking around, and until you commit a buy, you're a stranger. Even if the owner has nothing to hide, the owner may wish to keep secret the fact the business is about to be sold. If employees sense that the grip of the present owner is weakening, their morale may suffer. The quality of the products they produce or the way they deal with customers may be affected. Even worse, they may start job hunting.

There may be one way to convince a reluctant seller to agree to a looksee. In Chapter 11 we'll discuss the *letter of intent,* which is often signed before the prospective buyer becomes obligated to buy. You could write a provision into the letter of intent that legally prohibits you from disclosing to anyone anything you learn during the look-see. If you offer this to an otherwise reluctant seller, you may get a look-see.

If you're successful in getting a look-see, try to learn as much as you can. The owner may spend all of his or her time in the office behind a desk. Your time is better served in the plant or beside a driver as he makes deliveries or going around with a salesperson. In short, try to observe and learn about every facet of the business. It shouldn't take more than a week for you to determine whether the business is right for you.

CONSULTING AGREEMENTS

Tom Brown was lucky his seller agreed to stick around for a couple of weeks after the sale in order to show him the ropes. It should be obvious that, in almost any sale, the continued presence of the seller in the business for a period of time after the sale is important. A smooth transition may mean an uninterrupted stream of sales. A poor transition may result in deteriorating employee relations, lost customers, or unhappy suppliers.

Some businesses require the continued presence of the seller more than do others. Those businesses that rely on the personal contacts of the owner place a premium on the continued presence of the seller. If Tom Brown had bought a real estate brokerage business, two weeks probably wouldn't have been enough time for the seller to introduce Tom to the sales agents or familiarize him with the current real estate listings. A transitional period measured in months might have been required.

The required length of the transition period is determined by the answer to the following question: "What does the seller know that I don't?" If it takes just a few days or weeks to learn all the subtleties of the business and become acquainted with the customers and suppliers, the continued presence of the seller for these few days or weeks is all you'll need.

Every seller has at some point said to the buyer: "If you have any questions after you buy the business, just give me a call." At this point the seller may have the best of intentions. But after the sale is closed, the seller may decide that playing golf is far more interesting than dealing with you. After all, not dealing with the business's problems is why he sold the business in the first place.

The seller's promise to consult with you after the closing isn't good enough. If you feel you'll need the seller's continued presence for any period of time, you should put it in writing in the form of a consulting agreement. This should be prepared by your attorney because it should be airtight. Here's the hard part: *You should pay the seller for the seller's consulting services.* You get what you pay for. If you don't pay the seller for his continuing services, you won't get any services.

The agreement should specify the amount of time the seller will have to provide for you. You may want the seller to be present in the store or plant on a full-time basis during the first few days after the closing. Thereafter, the seller's presence a few hours a day may be sufficient. Still later, a requirement that the seller show up on an as-needed basis may be all you need. The agreement should also specify any particular duties you may want the seller to perform in addition to general consulting matters. For example, you may want the seller to call his suppliers and major customers, informing them of the sale and introducing them to you. You may even want the seller to accompany you when you go to meet with these suppliers and customers.

The best way to pay for the seller's consulting services is to back a specified amount out of the purchase price of the business and pay the amount only if and when the seller provides the services. For example, you might say to the seller: "We've agreed on a price of $100,000 for your business. I'll pay you $92,500 for the business, on terms to be negotiated, and $7,500 for three months' consulting services, payable $2,500 per month. As you perform the services in accordance with the consulting agreement, I'll pay you the $2,500 on the last day of each month." If the seller is really motivated to sell, he may have to cool his desire to get out quickly and agree to consult for three months.

Most sellers don't have a problem providing some consulting services. After the Tax Reform Act of 1986, they shouldn't have a problem reducing the purchase price of the business while getting paid for their services. With the repeal of the deduction for long-term capital gains treatment, there's no tax difference between being paid for stock and being paid for consulting services—it's all taxed to the seller as ordinary income.

NONCOMPETITION AGREEMENTS

How would you like to buy a business engaged in millwork operations only to have the seller open up another millwork business across the street, in direct competition with the business you've just bought? A pretty grim prospect, isn't it? You might assume that having just sold you his business, the last thing the seller would want to do is go back into the same line of work. It doesn't always work out that way. After spending a few months in Spain, Mr. Houston may realize that retirement isn't much fun and that building windows and doors is really where the action is.

The only sure way to prevent your seller from competing with you is to write a noncompetition agreement or to include a non-competition provision in the purchase agreement. When you suggest a noncompetition agreement to your seller, he may look at you as if you had taken leave of your senses; the bags may be packed and the tickets for sunny Spain may have been bought. Competing with you may be the last thing on the seller's mind. Don't accept the seller's assurances that reentering the type of business being sold is the last thing on the seller's mind. If the seller *truly* doesn't ever want to compete with you, you shouldn't have any difficulty obtaining the seller's consent.

A noncompetition agreement is the toughest thing your attorney will ever write. If the seller ever decides to go back into the same business, you'll have to sue the seller on the agreement and it had better hold up in court. A tough noncompetition agreement means that not only will the seller not be able to compete with you, he won't be able to compete with you *through anyone else*. This means prohibitng the seller from setting up a corporation owned by his or her spouse and acting as a consultant to that corporation.

Noncompetition isn't all the noncompetition agreement should provide for. If the business you're buying has any trade secrets or proprietary information, such as a customer list, the seller should be prohibited from *disclosing* the trade secrets or proprietary information to anyone, whether or not the seller actually starts competing with you. The wrongful sale or disclosure of your business's secrets to someone else could make your business less competitive or cause someone else to start competing with you.

Judges don't like noncompetition agreements. They're viewed as a form of slavery. Some states have laws limiting their use and enforceability. For this reason, it's essential to have an attorney draft the noncompetition agreement. If you have to enforce it, you'll want it to hold up.

Chapter 8
HOW TO BUY A FRANCHISE

JUST WHAT *IS* FRANCHISING?

The advertising motto of Holiday Inns is "The Best Surprise Is No Surprise." This really is the motto of every franchise operation; every one is premised on the fact that no matter where you go, you'll encounter uniformity (or at least *minimum standards*) of product and service. And to make sure you recognize the uniform products and services you'll receive, it's all wrapped up in nationally advertised names, trademarks, designs, and logos.

Let's say you're on a car trip from your home in Maine to California. While rolling down Interstate 80 just outside Omaha, you encounter two restaurants side by side. One is Sam's Diner; the other is McDonald's, complete with golden arches. The design of the McDonald's building looks just like the McDonald's restaurant around the corner from your home in Maine. In fact, *everything* looks the same, both on the inside and the outside. What do you know about Sam's Diner? Nothing. Sam may serve up the tastiest hamburgers in the United States, true triumphs of the culinary art, and at the fairest prices. On the other hand, Sam's hamburgers may kill you and you may get gypped in the process. You just don't know. You do, however, know quite a bit about the

McDonald's next to Sam's. You know pretty much what will be on the menu and roughly what it will cost. You even know what the food will *taste* like: exactly how it tasted in Maine. You also have a pretty good idea what the service will be like and how the rest room will look. Do you want adventure or do you want to make it to California? Will you try McDonald's, where they've sold 50 billion burgers, or Sam's, where they may not have sold fifty?

The essence of franchising, and the reason for its success, is to allow the buying public, never known for its spirit of adventure, to identify with a certain level of *uniformity* of product and service. Identification is made through a nationally (or regionally) advertised and promoted name. This name is reinforced by uniform trademarks, signs, building designs, uniforms, interior decorations, and anything else that can be standardized. When we think of franchise operations, we tend to think first of fast food outlets. But anything that can be standardized can be franchised, from real estate brokers to travel agencies to auto parts. Even *lawyers* can be franchisees!

The success of franchising in our society is a fact. From humble beginnings (Singer sold its sewing machines through authorized outlets in the nineteenth century) franchising has grown into an industry with *$500 billion* in annual sales, and only 10 percent of that is tied up in fast food. Close to 5 million people are employed in 466,000 franchised outlets and the numbers keep growing every year. Clearly, franchising is where the action is.

What, then, is franchising? It's a method of conducting business whereby one party (the *franchisor*) grants to another (the *franchisee*) the right to conduct business in accordance with the franchisor's prescribed methods under the franchisor's name and trademark. Franchising could not have succeeded to the extent it has unless there're benefits to both the franchisor and the franchisee. And there are—lots of them.

To the franchisor, franchising represents an ideal method for business expansion *at low cost*. Think of the cost entailed in expanding a business one outlet at a time, which is what large merchandisors did before franchising took hold. Also, think of the difference in motivation between that of a store manager in a chain and that of an owner of a local franchise. The store manager is paid a salary; the franchisee owner gets to keep the profits. As more and more franchises go into operation, the franchisor's name and trademark develop that much more clout, and the franchisor's advertising becomes that much more powerful. Nothing succeeds like success, and there's no success like a national franchise operation.

The benefits to the franchisee can be just as great. Let's go back to Sam's Diner, and the fellow next door operating under the McDonald's name. Sam may cook pretty good hamburgers, but he may not know beans about marketing, accounting, purchasing or personnel management. As a franchisee his franchisor may train him in all that. In our example, Sam at least has a location from where to sell his hamburgers, a grill on which to cook them, and tables on which to serve them. But if he doesn't, and still wants to sell hamburgers, his franchisor may find him a location, build the building (or negotiate a lease), and buy the equipment for him, or at least provide the financing to obtain the equipment. We've assumed that Sam knows how to make hamburgers. Perhaps he does, but he may not know how to make them uniformly and move them quickly. His franchisor may teach him that as well. Operating out of one location, Sam has to buy his ground beef, napkins, soda straws, and all the hundreds of other supplies that go into operating a restaurant dealing in small quantities. As a franchisee his franchisor may be able to get him lower prices by buying in huge quantities for all the franchisees.

And then there's that McDonald's name, and those golden arches. Sam won't have to worry about all the years it might otherwise take for word to get out that his hamburgers taste good and his prices are fair: other franchisees, and the franchisor's advertising, have long ago taken care of that. On the very first morning that Sam opens shop as a franchisee under an identifiable name, the customers should start coming in. Being a franchisee is no guarantee of riches. But if you pick the right franchisor, at least some of the heartache and frustration that go into starting a business will be eliminated.

There are, of course, disadvantages in being a franchisee. For starters, all that training and expertise the franchisor will supply you with will cost you, and the more established and recognized the product or service being franchised, the higher the price. To become a franchisee, you will most likely have to pay an initial franchise fee, either all in cash or part in cash and part down the road. You will also be obligated to pay to the franchisor a certain percentage of your monthly or quarterly *gross* revenues. This is a very important point to keep in mind: by being obligated to pay over a percentage of your gross, the franchisor will make money off your business even if you never turn a profit. You may also be obligated to pay certain other fees, such as your share of group advertising and marketing. And all that is on top of the normal costs of conducting a business.

There's another big disadvantage in being a franchisee, a disadvantage that makes franchising unacceptable to many people. Most people willingly undertake the risk of owning their own business as long as they know they're their own boss. As a franchisee you're not. Depending on the nature of the operation, there may be severe limitations on the manner in which you're allowed to conduct business. Let's take a look again at Sam's Diner and the fellow running the McDonald's next door. Sam can sell anything he wants any time he wants. If he wants to shut down on Thursdays to go fishing, he can. If he devises a new recipe for bean soup, he can try it out on his customers that evening. If his "accounting" system is a cash register and a shoe box, it's between Sam and the IRS, no one else. The floor can be as messy as his conscience and the Health Department, but no one else, will permit. And no one will tell him to be friendly to the customers!

It's a different story for the fellow next door running the McDonald's. He has to account to his franchisor for every cent earned. He has to count all the buns sold, all the ketchup consumed. Sam can fiddle with the recipes; a McDonald's franchisee can't. No one will meddle in Sam's operation; franchisors have a way of meddling all the time.

When you think of it, though, franchisors *should* meddle in the affairs of their franchisees; they should control their operations. Remember what we said: The very essence of franchising is uniformity of product or service. If you're operating a fast food franchise in Omaha, and the franchisees in St. Louis are selling bad food with poor service, it affects your franchise. Since the key lies in the public's acceptance of certain goods and services it associates with the name and trademark, the franchisor must maintain standards of quality in the delivery of the goods and services. A franchisor who doesn't do that isn't doing anything, and his franchise operation will soon suffer.

SELECTING THE RIGHT FRANCHISE

Evaluate Yourself

We spoke in Chapter 1 about the need to analyze your own strengths and weaknesses when buying any business. The things that you should consider when buying a business should also be considered when selecting a franchise. Is this franchise the type of business you'll be comfortable with? Do you have any personal conflicts with the methods or hours of operation of this particular franchise operation? Once again, analyzing yourself may be the most difficult thing you'll have to do. You may be told about, and may even meet, franchisees who've become very successful. But they may have been better equipped, either through training, education, motivation, or personality, to succeed at this particular operation. Digging deep within yourself is something only you can do; your lawyer and accountant can't help.

When considering a franchise, there're a number of things you have to ask yourself that need not be considered when buying a nonfranchised business. If you buy any other type of business, you know you'll be your own boss. If you buy a franchise, you'll, to a greater or lesser extent, be monitored and controlled by someone else. To an extent you'll take orders from an outside organization, your franchisor. Your discretion will be limited as to the products you can sell or the methods by which you conduct business. How do you feel about that? If you want as much freedom as possible, choose a franchise that grants you this freedom. If you want or need direction and can use the accounting, marketing, and personnel management help many franchisors offer, choose a franchise at that end of the spectrum.

Franchises fall within two broad classifications. The *business format franchise* offers a full range of accounting, training, and management services along with the controls that go with them. Fast food operations fall into this category. The *product and service franchise* allows you to sell or distribute a product or service under a name and trademark with less training, assistance, and control. Most distributorships fall into this category. There are gradations of assistance and control within each class. How much control you can handle and how much help you think you'll need are decisions only you can make.

How to Find a Franchise

If you think franchising is for you, you won't have much trouble finding franchises for sale. Franchisors advertise extensively in business publications and newspapers. You may also find franchising fairs or conventions in your area, where numerous franchisors exhibit their operations. Your local bookstore or library should have a number of books, such as the *Franchise Opportunities Handbook,* which lists most of the franchise operations in business today, categorized by industry.

The best way to select a franchise operation, however, is to contact a franchise broker. Since franchising itself is relatively new, and franchise brokerage is newer, there may not be a franchise broker in your area, but there should be at least one in most large cities. To find a franchise broker in your area, check with the International Franchise Association, 1025 Connecticut Avenue, NW, Washington, DC 20036. You should remember, however, that franchise brokers represent *franchisors,* and it's their job to find franchisees for their clients. Nevertheless, a reputable franchise broker will work hard to assure that the right person is married to the right franchisor. Most franchisors (especially established ones) prefer it that way.

Start-Up and Established Franchisors

Every established franchise operation, even McDonald's, started out by selling its *first* franchise to somebody. The question is whether you'd prefer to be the first, third, or fifth franchisee of a start-up operation or the three-thousandth or five-thousandth franchisee of an established franchisor.

The risks inherent in buying a franchise from a start-up franchisor are obvious. Since the essence of franchising is the public's awareness and acceptance of the franchisor's name and products or services, buying into a start-up operation carries the risk that the public won't accept the franchisor's products or services or that its acceptance will be too slow and lukewarm for you to generate a profit. Since the start-up franchisor needs to develop franchises quickly in order to roll out his operation, the franchisor may be more willing to accept marginally qualified (or unqualified) people to be his franchisees than would an established franchisor. The franchisor may even need the franchise fee paid to buy a franchise just to keep going. If the other franchisees foul up in their operations, it will affect your franchise. With a long-established franchisor, you're more secure in the knowledge that the public's acceptance of the product or service is not just a passing fancy. If you're the first franchisee selling a hot new computer service, you may be in on the ground floor of something that may be around forever or may be gone in a year.

An even more fundamental question that must be answered by any startup franchisor is whether he or she has a product or service that can be franchised at all. Here's an example: I once had a client, whom I'll call Frank, who was thinking about franchising his moderately successful hot dog restaurant. The restaurant had a catchy name and a registered trademark. The hot dogs were good, but the manufacturer who sold to Frank would sell to anyone who would buy them. When I visited the restaurant, I was most taken by what I *didn't* see. Frank sold hot dogs the same way most anyone would sell them: from behind a counter, standing in front of a large menu. The menu indicated that Frank also sold hamburgers, sandwiches, pizza, and even beer and wine. The restaurant had no particular theme and no unusual or unique way of selling. There was nothing different about the decor or the design of the store. What I *did* notice was that Frank had a way with customers; he greeted and started up a conversation with almost everyone who waited in line. Frank was always cheerful and that made the customers cheerful. But what could Frank offer to someone who operated under his name and trademark? Not much. And that's the point. Not every successful business, even a fast food business, can be franchised. Only those businesses whose products, services, or methods can be transferred to others but that cannot be easily duplicated can be franchised. With a start-up operation you often don't know if the business is one that fits.

There're advantages, however, in buying into a start-up franchise operation. Without question, the cost of buying an unproven franchise will be lower (perhaps *far* lower) than of buying a franchise in a nationwide operation where there're hundreds of successful franchisees. If you're one of the first franchisees in a start-up operation, you'll have a greater opportunity to negotiate the terms of the franchise agreement, which will govern your relations with the franchisor. In an established franchise operation the terms of the franchise agreement are pretty much take it or leave it; your franchise agreement will be exactly like hundreds of others.

Most important, as one of the first of a franchisor's franchisees, your franchisor *needs you to succeed.* You may be showered with attention, receiving far more tender loving care than you might receive from an established franchisor where you're a face in the crowd. An established franchisor may terminate your franchise quickly if you screw up; a start-up franchisor may need to keep you going.

The key then (and this should come as no surprise) is *know your franchisor.* Is the franchisor interested in seeing you succeed, or is the franchisor primarily interested in getting a franchise fee? Fortunately, *finding out* about a franchisor is easier than finding out about the seller of a nonfranchised business.

Evaluating the Franchisor

The Franchise Disclosure Document

When franchising was just becoming popular in the 1960s, a small army of franchisors emerged who ran the gamut from the well-meaning but incompetent to the out-and-out crooked. They promised assistance in starting a business, promised training and counseling, took the franchise fee, and were gone. They employed high-pressure sales techniques, making inflated or phony claims about their past success and their future intentions. For a while they threatened to bring all of franchising down around them.

Just as hordes of carpetbaggers selling bogus stock certificates eventually led to the creation of the Securities and Exchange Commission and the passage of numerous state and federal securities laws, unscrupulous franchise salesmen were bound to bring on the regulators. In 1971 California passed the first law regulating the sale of franchises and other states followed. In 1979 the Federal Trade Commission (FTC) issued a rule governing the sale of franchises, nationwide. The principal result was that if anyone in the United States is offered a franchise, the prospective franchisee must receive *at least ten days prior to signing a franchise agreement or paying any money* a disclosure document, which in most states is called a Uniform Franchise Offering Circular (UFOC). The various states are permitted to pass laws making the disclosure required in the UFOC *tougher* than what the FTC requires, but no state can lessen the disclosure requirements. The requirement that you receive a disclosure document is one great advantage over buying a nonfranchised business. When you buy a business from a seller, you'll have to ferret out for yourself all the information you'll need to make an intelligent decision. Before you buy a franchise, the franchisor will have to give you that information.

All disclosure documents are lengthy. They're difficult and expensive for franchisors to prepare. Let's look at some of the things a franchisor must tell you about his operation before you buy.

1. *The name and address of the franchisor and any predecessors.* If you find that your franchisor was incorporated only this year, but did business under another name in another state last year, and under still another name the year before that, it may be a tip-off that the franchisor's past has been rocky. If the franchisor is very new or has been changing identity, keep digging.

2. *The franchisor's business experience, the length of time that business has been conducted, and the type of business operated.* Here the franchisor must disclose how long the franchisor has actually been conducting business and exactly what the franchise operation is all about.

3. *The numbers of other franchises sold, the time they have been for sale, and the identity of other franchisors.* This is where you learn (if you don't know already) how established or start-up the operation is. The franchisor must furnish for you the names and addresses of ten franchisees in your area or *all* the franchisees if there are fewer than ten.

4. *The identity and experience of all the franchisor's officers and affiliates.* Here you can gauge if the franchisor knows what he's doing and whether he can deliver. If it's a start-up operation offering franchises for the sale of computer equipment, you'd like to see whether the officers of, principal employees of, or consultants to the franchisor have extensive (or any) experience in computers. The UFOC requires that the occupations and employment of each of them be described for the five-year period preceding the offering.

5. *Litigation.* Has the franchisor been sued? (*By his own franchisees*)? If the franchisor has been sued or is suing others, particularly his own franchisees, you *must* find out why. The UFOC requires a brief description of what each lawsuit is all about. If the description doesn't satisfy you, get your lawyer to dig out more facts.

6. *Bankruptcy.* If the franchisor, any of its predecessors, or any of its officers has ever gone through bankruptcy, it's a tip-off they

may not be very adept in business or in handling money. Do you want to invest your savings and your future with someone who has gone down the drain before?

7. *Initial fees and other payments.* The franchisor will have to tell you exactly how much you'll have to pay, when, and to whom. Obviously this will include an initial fee as well as any royalty payments you will be required to make. If you'll also be required to buy inventory or equipment or pay into an advertising budget, these payments too must be specifically described.

8. *Franchisee's initial investment.* The franchisor is required to provide you with a summary of what the franchisor estimates it will take to get into business, whether or not the payments are made to the franchisor. Remember, these are only estimates. If you have a problem with any of it, challenge the estimates.

9. *Required purchases or leases from the franchisor.* Will the franchisor require you to buy certain goods or lease certain equipment from the franchisor? Often franchisees are delighted to buy from the franchisor, since the franchisor is often able to buy in bulk or sell at a reduced rate if the franchisor itself is a manufacturer. But often franchisees find they can buy cheaper elsewhere and are prevented from doing so. If the franchisor doesn't require you to buy from him but has specifications only a set of approved suppliers can meet, these specifications must also be described.

10. *Financing arrrangements.* If the franchisor is going to help you get into business by financing your inventory, equipment, or the store itself, you'll have to know the terms. The financing you get from your franchisor may not be competitive with the financing you could arrange yourself. You should prepare the same type of pro forma for a franchise that you would prepare to purchase any business, and the terms of the financing will have to be plugged in.

11. *The franchisor's obligations to train, assist, or provide other services.* This may be why you are buying a franchise in the first place. Everything the franchisor says he will do for you has to be spelled out.

12. *Exclusive territory.* If you're going to sell the franchisor's products and services, it would be nice to know that the franchisor won't sell another franchise across the street. If you're to be granted an exclusive territory, it must be described in detail. Also, the franchisor will have to disclose whether or not the franchisor has or reserves the right to establish *company-owned* stores that might compete with you.

13. *Description of trademarks and patents.* Your franchise may be only as valuable as the franchisor's trademark or patent. The franchisor must disclose to you whether or not the trademark or patent has been nationally registered and whether he knows of any possible infringement his patent or trademark has made on someone else's patent or trademark. If someone has claimed that it does, you must be told. If the franchisor does (or doesn't) plan to defend you if *you* are sued for patent or trademark infringement, this needs to be disclosed.

14. *Restriction on goods or services you can sell.* Let's say the franchisor offers three products for sale. You may think (or learn later) that two of the products can sell but that the third will be nailed to the shelf. Will the franchisor require you to sell *all* his products? Either way, you have to be told.

15. *Possibility of renewal, termination, or repurchase of the franchise.* This may be the most important section of the disclosure document. It certainly is the one that causes the most lawsuits between franchisors and their franchisees. The number of franchisees who have invested their life savings and years of their lives in a franchise only to have the franchisor terminate their right to use the trademark and cut off supplies are too numerous to mention. Franchisors have the right under certain circumstances to terminate a franchisee. If a franchisee is mistreating the public, either by poor service or nonconforming products, every franchisee and the well-being of the entire operation may suffer. But a disreputable franchisor may wish to terminate a successful franchisee, even if the franchisee has done nothing wrong, just to take over the franchise and either run it as a company operation or resell it to someone else. Even if the franchise is not terminated by the

actions of the franchisor, franchises usually don't last forever; they *expire*. You must ascertain what your rights are to renew the franchise once it expires.

Renewal and termination clauses are often drafted by franchisors for their benefit or at best are purposefully vague. Your lawyer should read the entire disclosure document, paying particular attention to the provisions dealing with the termination, renewal, or repurchase of the franchise.

16. *Projected Sales and Profits.* The franchisor must estimate for you what the franchisor believes you can do in the way of sales and profits. These projections must, however, be based on something; they cannot have been pulled out of a hat. For example, the franchisor must tell you how many of the other franchisees have met or exceeded the projections. Show the projections to your accountant. If your accountant has concerns with any of the figures, you and your accountant should sit down with the franchisor and go over them. Don't take what you get at face value.

This describes most, but not all, of the things about the franchisor you must be shown. But a word of caution about the disclosure document. The FTC requires only that the franchisor prepare the document and show it to you. The FTC doesn't read it; it doesn't even receive it. Some states* do require that the disclosure document be registered with their department of corporations or another state agency. But even in these states the regulatory authority usually will be interested only in whether the franchisor has made all the disclosures required by law; it doesn't check whether the disclosures are *true*. Also, the regulating authority usually doesn't care whether the franchise you're being offered is a good deal. If the disclosure document fully describes a deal in which you're not likely to make money, that's your problem, not theirs.

There's no substitute for you and your lawyer and accountant

*California, Hawaii, Illinois, Indiana, Maryland, Michigan, Minnesota, New York, North Dakota, Oregon, Rhode Island, South Dakota, Virginia, Washington, and Wisconsin.

going through the disclosure document (and the franchise agreement and financial statements that must accompany it), analyzing it, and picking it apart. I've been amazed by the number of franchisees who invest their time and savings, relying only on sales pitches, who *never read the disclosure document!*

Evaluate the Salesperson

There's one surefire way to tell if your franchisor wants you to succeed as a franchisee or wants only to collect a franchise fee: A high-pressure sales pitch is a dead giveaway. If a salesperson (or an officer of the franchisor) tries to put the arm on you, take a hike. If the salesperson tries to sell you on the deal before giving you the disclosure document or tries to get a check from you too quickly (assuring you that it will be placed in escrow or not cashed and you can "get it back any time") you're dealing with an operation that wants franchise fees, not successful franchisees. Remember, the same high-pressure tactics being employed on you are being employed on everyone else, so that no prospective franchisee is being checked for proper qualifications. How successful can a franchise operation be if the franchisor will take anyone? On the other hand, if the franchisor's representative wants to see your financial statement, if you have to disclose your background in business or whether you've ever filed for bankruptcy, you're dealing with a franchisor who's being careful and selective with *all* prospective franchisees. Here's a good rule of thumb: The care and prudence the franchisor evidences in *selecting* franchisees will carry over and govern the care the franchisor employs in dealing with franchisees after they've signed on.

Contact Other Franchisees

There's no substitute for contacting the other franchisees in your area before you decide to buy. Before you visit them, read the disclosure document carefully. Make a list of all the things the franchisor promises will be done for you and any other concerns you have either from your reading of the document, from your meetings with the salesperson, or from any other source. Then contact as many franchisees as will meet with you. (Remember, their names and addresses are right there in the document.) Visit the franchisees *at their businesses*. Try to get a feel for what it's like to operate a franchise, put yourself in the franchisees' shoes.

Ask tough, specific questions. If the disclosure document mentions a training program or a personnel manual, ask about whether the training was sufficient and the manuals provided were adequate. There may be a wealth of information that never found its way into the disclosure document. Are deliveries made on time? Are subtle pressures employed to get franchisees to participate in "voluntary" test-marketing programs? These and a host of other questions about the *operations* of the franchise can be answered only by the franchisees. Make certain the franchisor's estimates of what it will take to start a franchise are reasonably accurate. You don't want to start operations undercapitalized, having to scramble for additional funds in order to stay in business or conduct business properly.

The franchisees will most likely speak freely with you about their experiences. Those who've done well will be proud to relate their success, those who haven't will want to unburden themselves. Along those lines, try to contact *former* franchisees, either those who've sold their franchises or, worse, those who've been terminated by the franchisor. Compare the franchisees who are satisfied with those who are not. There may be one factor or a small number of factors that distinguish the successful from the unsuccessful franchisees. For example, you may find the only franchises that succeed are run by a married couple. The nature of the business may be such that only if there's one person out in front dealing with the customers and another in the back (baking doughnuts, stuffing envelopes, or whatever) can the business be operated successfully. If you're a single person who has to *hire* another person, this may not be the franchise for you. Whomever you speak to, ask them if they would do it all over again, knowing what they now know.

Do not, however, visit a franchisee who's been in business only a short time. The glow hasn't worn off. He or she may not yet even be in a position to know if the operation will be profitable.

After you've spoken to as many present and former franchisees as you can, reread the disclosure document. How much does it contain that simply isn't true? How much have you learned about the franchise that it doesn't contain?

A Final Word

In some cases the franchisor will promise to build, lease, or furnish a store for you. The franchisor may promise that the completed and stocked business will be ready for operation by a certain date. *Never quit your job or shut down your present business until you're certain that your franchise is ready to start business.* There're lots of delays in life. Don't let them cost you money.

Chapter 9

CHOOSING THE FORM IN WHICH TO CONDUCT BUSINESS

The seller may be conducting business in one of a number of ways. The business may now be in the form of a sole proprietorship, a general partnership, or a limited partnership, or it may be run as a corporation, either as a regular corporation or an S corporation. Unless you decide (or are required as a result of the negotiations) to buy the stock of an existing corporation, you'll be free to choose the form in which you wish to conduct your business.

Let's analyze the advantages and disadvantages inherent in each form of business from the following perspectives:

1. Ease of operation.
2. Management and control of the business.
3. Transferability of ownership interests.
4. Extent of liability placed on the owners.
5. Taxation of the business and its owners.
6. Ability to raise capital.

Before we explore how each form of business measures up, let's summarize what each form of business is.

THE SOLE PROPRIETORSHIP

If you go into business without doing anything else (i.e., without forming a partnership or a corporation), you're a sole proprietor. It's certainly the quickest, easiest, and cheapest way to start a business; most people who make some money on the side are sole proprietors. For example, a woman who knits sweaters in her spare time and sells them at local flea markets is likely to be a sole proprietor.

Being a sole proprietor doesn't mean, however, that you have to work alone. A sole proprietorship can, and aften does, have employees. It just means that the business has only one *owner,* who makes all the decisions. Neither does operating as a sole proprietor mean that you have to operate the business under your own name. If the woman who knits sweaters in her spare time wants to sell her sweaters under the label ''Fancy Knits,'' she can do so. All she needs to do is comply with the local law governing the protection of names, usually by filing a *trade name affidavit* with the county clerk or secretary of state. If the name is available, she, and no one else, will be able to use the name. However, in most states a sole proprietor can protect the name only in the county in which the business is conducted; corporations can protect their names on a statewide basis.

THE GENERAL PARTNERSHIP

A partnership (general or limited) is defined by the Uniform Partnership Act as ''as association of two or more persons to carry on a business as co-owners for profit.'' A general partnership, which is one that has two or more ''general'' partners, is, at least theoretically, as easy to form as a sole proprietorship. You don't need to have anything in writing to form one, and you don't need to file anything with the state or local government. As with a sole proprietorship, if the partners want to conduct business under a trade name, they can file a trade name affidavit in the county or counties in which they intend to do business.

It's so easy to form a general partnership that you can be a partner in a general partnership without knowing it! As long as two or more people carry on a business as co-owners for profit, they're partners. An example: Let's say two people decide to rent out a computer and split rental payments. One of them owns the computer; the other services it. When the computer is sold, they split the proceeds. They may never think of themselves as partners in a general partnership, yet they are.

THE LIMITED PARTNERSHIP

A limited partnership is in many ways the same, but in some important aspects radically different from, the general partnership. Like a general partnership, a limited partnership has at least two partners, who carry on a business as co-owners for profit. At least one of the partners is a *general partner,* just as in a general partnership, and at least one of the partners is a *limited partner.* A limited partner, however, doesn't have any right to manage the affairs of the partnership. He or she is prohibited by law from having anything but the most rudimentary management rights, and if he attempts to exercise any management rights, he becomes a general partner. The trade-off for not having any management rights is that the limited partner is also relieved of any liabilities beyond his own investment in the partnership. For example, if a limited partner invests $5,000 in a limited partnership and somebody sues the partnership for $1,000,000, the most the limited partner can lose is $5,000; the general partner is on the hook for the rest.

A limited partnership is more difficult to form then a general partnership, and you can't be in a limited partnership without knowing it. To form a limited partnership, you must file a certificate with your secretary of state or county clerk. Depending on state law, the certificate will have to spell out all the rights of the partners, how much money they invested, what business the partnership will conduct, and a host of other particulars. If the certificate doesn't comply with the state law, the secretary of state or county clerk won't accept the certificate.

As we'll see shortly, the limited partnership combines some of the best tax features of a general partnership, and for the limited partners, some of the best features of a corporation with respect to limitations on liability.

THE CORPORATION

Every lawyer knows that a corporation is a *separate legal entity*. This means that if there are two people, Jones and Brown, sitting in a room and they form a corporation, Jones & Brown, Inc., in the eyes of the law there are three "people" sitting in the room. The corporation has an existence separate and apart from its owners, Jones and Brown. Neither Jones or Brown are the ones who sell any goods, provide any services, or make any money; Jones & Brown, Inc. does all that. The corporation can sue in its own name as well as be sued. The corporation, and not Jones or Brown, enters into contracts, hires employees, signs leases, and the like. Most important, the corporation, not Jones or Brown, pays taxes on its earnings. The corporation is a separate taxpayer, filing its own tax return on the money it makes. The separate nature of the corporation is the key to all the advantages (and some disadvantages) of setting up a corporation to conduct a business.

Just as you can't be a partner in a limited partnership without knowing it, you can't be a shareholder in a corporation without knowing it. To form a corporation, you must file a certificate, called "Articles of Incorporation" in most states, with the secretary of state, who charters your corporation. (Some corporations, such as federal banks, are chartered by the federal government). The certificate will also require you to include information about the business you intend to conduct, the rights of the shareholders, and so forth.

By filing a certificate with the secretary of state, you protect your corporate name on a statewide basis. In some cases merely protecting the name statewide is reason enough to incorporate. If you decide you don't want to conduct your business under your *corporate* name, or decide later on that you want to do business under a different name than that of your corporation, it's no problem. A corporation can also file a trade name affidavit, under which it protects (usually on a statewide basis) the name under which it operates. A word of caution: No state will grant you a name that is the same, or very similar, to a name already in use. If

you plan to do business in more than one state, check with the
Secretary of State of *both* states that the name is available.

Corporations are either closely held or public in nature, with
most public corporations starting out as closely held (or close) corporations. A close corporation has few shareholders, and there is
likely to be little or no public market for the shares. Public corporations are often owned by hundreds, or even thousands, of shareholders, whose shares are freely traded by brokers on national or
regional stock exchanges. Close corporations are usually unregu-
lated unless the corporation engages in a business regulated by a
state or federal authority, such as a state liquor authority or the
Federal Aviation Agency. Public companies are always regulated
by the Securities and Exchange Commission (SEC), which exacts
a heavy burden of compliance, requiring complete and thorough
reporting on operations and finances. The business you will buy
will likely be a close corporation.

Who's Who: Shareholders, Directors, and Officers

There's a lot of confusion regarding who's who in a corporation.
As an owner of a closely held corporation, you're likely to wear a
number of hats simultaneously. You'll undoubtedly be a shareholder, if not the sole shareholder. You'll probably also be a director and an officer, probably the president. Let's see what each of
these hats means.

The shareholders (also termed the ''stockholders'') are the
owners of a corporation. If you're the sole owner, you own 100
percent of the *issued* stock. Every corporation must have at least
one class of stock, and if you only have one class, it's *common* stock.
Many corporations have classes of *preferred* stock, which give their
holders preferences with respect to the receipt of dividends or the
division of proceeds when the corporation is liquidated. Often the
holders of preferred stock are denied voting rights, so they don't
have a voice in the management of the corporation, in much the
same fashion as a limited partner in a limited partnership. The
shareholders, who have the voting rights (usually the *common*
shareholders), *elect* the board of directors.

The directors who serve on the board of directors have the legal responsibility to run the corporation. Technically, it's the directors who make the management decisions. If the corporation commits fraud, or if it wastes investors' money, very often it's the directors who are sued. The board of directors *appoints* the officers.

The officers, usually the president, vice president, treasurer, and secretary, have the day-to-day responsibility to run the business. This arrangement can be diagrammed as follows:

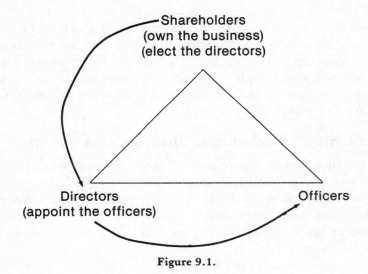

Figure 9.1.

There's a reason the shareholders are at the apex of the pyramid. Since the shareholders elect the directors, who appoint the officers, it's the shareholders who run the show, as it should be, since they own the corporation. If you're the sole owner of the corporation (owning 100 percent of the shares) and there are ten directors, have you given up any control of the corporation? Not at all. If the other nine directors don't do as you want, you can call a shareholders' meeting (you'll be the only person in attendance) and fire them all!

What all this means is that in a close corporation, being a shareholder is everything and being a director or officer means next to nothing. Moreover, the number of shares you own doesn't mean anything either; it's your *percentage* of shares that counts. All this goes somewhat against the natural instinct. After all, what would you rather be, the president of General Motors or just a GM shareholder? Isn't it better to own 100,000 shares of General Motors than 100 shares? It is, because every share of General Motors carries with it the right to receive a dividend check every three months. Close corporations, however, don't (and as we'll soon see, *shouldn't*) pay dividends. In a close corporation where there're only two shareholders, there's little difference (except for the rights to the proceeds on liquidation) between being a 1 percent shareholder and a 49 percent shareholder; each will give you the right to lose on every matter voted on by the shareholders, including voting on directors. By the same token, there's little difference between being a 51 percent shareholder and a 100 percent shareholder. With 51 percent of the voting power you're in control for all purposes. Owners of close corporations often get into a tizzy as to who the directors and officers will be. Don't worry about it; 51 percent of the stock is all you need.

THE S CORPORATION

There's really no such thing as an S corporation, which until recently was called a "Subchapter S corporation." An S corporation is formed in the same way as a regular corporation. It has the same shareholders, directors, and officers and conducts its business the same way. There's one, and only one, difference. By filing an election with the IRS under Subchapter S of the Internal Revenue Code, the corporation is *not* taxed as a separate entity. Rather, it's taxed almost exactly as a general partnership. We'll see what this entails a little later.

Having summarized what each form of business is all about, let's see how each one measures up.

EASE OF OPERATION

The sole proprietorship is the easiest way to operate a business. You aren't required to file anything with anyone (except for applicable licenses) or report to anyone. *You* make all the decisions. In fact, the best way to think of a sole proprietorship is that, for *all* purposes, there's no difference between the business and the person who owns the business.

A general partnership is as easy to run as a sole proprietorship. You also don't have to report to anyone. If the partners agree on decisions, the decisions are made, without the necessity of meetings, minutes, or reports.

A corporation (be it a regular corporation or an S corporation) isn't nearly as easy to operate. As we've seen, you'll need to file a full set of articles of incorporation or a detailed certificate just to get started. Some states, such as Texas, require that the corporation have a minimum amount of capital at the outset. Thereafter, depending on state law, you'll be required to file periodic reports to the secretary of state, providing such information as to who your directors, officers, and shareholders are. You'll also have to hold periodic shareholders' and directors' meetings. Often a bank or other party you'll want to deal with will require proof that the corporation (which, remember, is a *separate legal person* from its owners) is empowered to take the action you want it to take, such as borrowing money. This will require you to prepare directors' or shareholders' minutes authorizing the transaction. There is, of course, another document the corporation will have to prepare that an unincorporated sole proprietorship won't: a corporate *tax return,* which is due whether or not the corporation makes any money. None of this is particularly difficult. Suffice it to say that if you decide to incorporate, your legal and accounting fees are bound to go up.

In some respects the limited partnership is the most difficult to operate. Most states have the same filing and reporting requirements for limited partnerships that they do for corporations but with one irksome addition: everytime there's a transfer of an ownership interest in a limited partnership, the certificate has to be amended in order to effect the change. This isn't true of corporations.

To summarize: The sole proprietorship is the easiest way to operate a business. (However, as we'll soon see, this may be its *only* advantage.) General partnerships are also easy to operate; corporations and limited partnerships are more difficult. But remember, none of the things you'll be required to do in *any* form of business is particularly burdensome; it shouldn't affect your choice.

MANAGEMENT AND CONTROL

The sole proprietorship affords the owner the easiest vehicle for operating a business. As a sole proprietor you're the *only* person authorized to make business decisions, no matter how many employees you have. You don't share management authority with anyone. The same is almost true with a limited partnership. If a limited partnership has one general partner and a hundred limited partners, only the general partner will make business decisions. Most states do, however, grant limited partners some rights, at the very least the right to receive periodic financial information about partnership operations.

We've already touched on the management of a corporation. Unless your state has a law that treats close corporations specially, you'll have to operate the business in the same way that General Motors does: through shareholders' and directors' meetings, appropriate resolutions, and all the rest. Again, these formalities are not difficult to comply with.

It's in the general partnership that we encounter a unique and troublesome problem. Each general partner is empowered by law to manage the partnership on an equal footing with the other partners. Each partner is an *agent* of the partnership, with the power to bind the partnership by his or her actions. Let's assume Mr. Brown is one of four general partners in the ABCD Partnership. Without informing his partners he entered into a contract for equipment with a supplier. Can the supplier enforce the contract, requiring the partnership to take the equipment and pay for it? Yes, it can, because as the agent of the partnership with full management rights, Mr. Brown had the authority to enter into the contract and bind the partnership. You can imagine the problems involved in a sixty-person partnership, with each partner having the power to enter into contracts on behalf of the partnership! A partial solution to the problem is to enter into a partnership agreement, which limits the powers of all partners and perhaps expands the powers of certain other (managing) partners. This is only a partial solution, since the existence of a partnership agreement won't solve your problem with the supplier who wants to be paid; having dealt in good faith with a partner who *exceeded* his authority, the supplier can enforce the agreement.

In sum, here is the problem of management and control that every general partnership faces: While business decisions in a sole proprietorship are centralized in the sole owner, and in the general partner in a limited partnership, and in the board of directors in a corporation, within a general partnership, authority is not centralized at all; every partner has it.

TRANSFERABILITY OF OWNERSHIP INTERESTS

If you're just now contemplating getting into a business, you may not be thinking of some day getting out. But it's worth a look.

We saw there's no difference between a sole proprietor and his business. This means that when a sole proprietor dies, his business dies with him. It also means it's impossible to break off a piece of the business and sell it to others.

It's only slightly easier to transfer a partner's interest in a general partnership. The important thing to note is that you *cannot* transfer your partnership management rights, even if you do manage to sell your interest in partnership profits. If you do sell your partnership interest, the only way your buyer will obtain your management rights is if the other partners agree to it, which makes for a new partnership.

As a shareholder in a corporation or as a limited partner, you're free to sell your corporate shares or your limited partnership interest, assuming anyone will buy it. (Remember what we said about how valuable it is to own 49 percent of the stock of a corporation that will never pay dividends.) If you want to prevent a stranger from becoming a shareholder in your business, you should provide for that in a shareholders' agreement.

EXTENT OF LIABILITY PLACED ON THE OWNERS

Let's assume you own a doughnut delivery business and one of the drivers of the delivery trucks you own operates the truck negligently, causing a serious injury to a pedestrian. The pedestrian (who becomes the plaintiff shortly after visiting his lawyer) sues your business and wins. Not only that, the pedestrian, who was badly injured and who had a convincing lawyer, wins a judgment for $1 million. Obtaining a judgment is not necessarily equivalent to *collecting* one. Let's look at the plaintiff's options.

If your business is a sole proprietorship, the plaintiff can most definitely get at the trucks, the cash, the furniture, even the doughnuts in order to satisfy the $1 million judgment. If there aren't $1 million in the business to cover the judgment, can the plaintiff also get his hands on your personal car, your home, your golf clubs? Sad to say, the plaintiff can. Remember, there's no difference between a sole proprietor and his business; they're one and the same. *Unlimited liability,* therefore, is the major disadvantage, and risk, in doing business in the form of a sole proprietorship.

Let's change the facts and assume that the doughnut delivery business is run by a general partnership. After the plaintiff is awarded the $1 million judgment, can the plaintiff go after the personal assets of each of the general partners? Yes! because each general partner has unlimited liability. The plaintiff will first have to try to collect from the partnership's assets, but if these aren't sufficient, each of the general partners is in trouble. What's worse, the plaintiff is not limited to collecting the judgment from each partner in the proportion of his partnership interest. If you're only one of four partners, each having a 25 percent interest, the plaintiff can still go after your personal assets for the full $1 million. You may then have a lawsuit against your three other partners for their share, but if they don't have the money, can't be found (not uncommon after big judgments are awarded), or have gone into bankruptcy (also not uncommon), you're left holding the bag. Unlimited liability is the major disadvantage of doing business as a general partnership.

What if the business is owned by a limited partnership? If the limited partnership doesn't have sufficient assets to pay the $1 million, can the plaintiff go against the general partner's assets? He or she certainly can. In fact, the general partner is the *only* partner the plaintiff can go against (assuming there's only one general partner), since the plaintiff can't go against the limited partners; the very essence of their status as limited partners is their *limited* liability.

Now let's assume that the doughnut delivery business is owned by a corporation. Can the plaintiff go against the assets of the corporation to collect the $1 million? The plaintiff can, since the *corporation* is responsible for the injury, even if it was committed by one of its employees. If the assets of the corporation are insufficient to pay the judgment, can the plaintiff go against the assets of the corporation's shareholders, directors, or officers? No! The *limited* liability of a corporation's owners is one of the key advantages in conducting business in corporate form.

Limited liability does not mean, however, that shareholders can walk away from any and all of the debts and liabilities of the corporation. Let's take a look at all of the things that limited liability *doesn't* do.

For one, incorporating your business won't insulate you from the debts and liabilities you incur before you incorporate. More important, since all banks, landlords, suppliers, and many others know that a corporation's owners have limited liability, they won't lend money or enter into leases or contracts with a corporation, especially a start-up business, unless its owners *guarantee* the payment of the debt in their personal capacities. In such an event, which you are likely to encounter frequently, limited liability won't help.

There're a few other exceptions to the limited liability of the owner of a corporation. Certain states have laws that make the principal shareholders personally liable for the wages owed to employees; if the corporation doesn't pay the wages it owes, the employee can sue the shareholders. Also, if the corporation fails in its responsibility to turn over to the Treasury withheld income taxes, Social Security, and unemployment compensation from its employees paychecks and the corporation goes bankrupt, the IRS has the authority to go after the shareholders, officers, and directors of the corporation for these monies.

Let's go back to the plaintiff with the $1 million judgment who can't satisfy it from the corporation's assets. There's one important exception to the general rule that the owners have limited liability. This is where the plaintiff is able to pierce the corporate veil, as the lawyers say, and attack the owners directly. The theory behind allowing the plaintiff to pierce the veil is that if the owners didn't treat their business as a corporation (i.e., as a *separate entity*), the corporation's existence won't be respected when the plaintiff comes to collect. Let's assume that after the owners of the doughnut delivery business formed their corporation, they effectively forgot they were incorporated. They never issued shares of stock and never elected directors or officers, or having done so, never conducted the required meetings. They commingled the corporation's assets with their personal assets or never had any corporate assets. In such a situation the "corporation" looks an awful lot like a sole proprietorship or a partnership. Under the theory that if it walks like a duck and quacks like a duck, it's a duck, a court will disregard the corporation and allow the plaintiff to go after the owners for their individual assets. The lesson here is that after you do incorporate, you should be careful to maintain the corporate formalities of holding annual shareholders' and directors' meetings at least annually, titling assets in the corporate name, and having a sufficient amount of assets in the corporation to pay recurring corporate liabilities.

By now you've probably realized that even if a sole proprietorship or partnership gets hit with a $1 million judgment, it's likely that the problem, or most problems of this nature, can be mitigated by insurance. In fact, we've come to the point in our society where the risk of almost any loss can be covered by insurance. This lessens the advantage of limited liability for a corporation, but it doesn't eliminate it. Insurance policies have been known to lapse or have gaps in coverage. Insurance companies have been known to refuse to cover certain events or cancel the coverage of bad risks. Although insurance should be considered for every form of business, including the corporation, and is a necessity for the unincorporated business, insurance is not a complete substitute for the advantage of limited liability afforded by doing business as a corporation.

TAXATION OF THE BUSINESS AND ITS OWNERS

Sole Proprietorships

We started out by saying that a sole proprietorship is indistinguishable from its owner. This fact carries through when we consider how the sole proprietorship is taxed. If Mrs. Brown, in the business of knitting sweaters under the name "Fancy Knits," earns a dollar on January 1, or December 31, or any day in between, it's income to *her*. Any valid business expense she incurs is also deductible by her, on Schedule C of her individual tax return (Form 1040.) In short, there's no *tax* difference between owning a business and getting a paycheck; you're taxed personally on what you receive between January 1 and December 31. There're *no* tax planning opportunities. But there's one advantage in being taxed directly: If you lose money in business in any year, the losses you show on your Schedule C will offset any other income you (or your spouse, if you file a joint return) have during the year.

General Partnerships and Limited Partnerships

In one important respect a general partnership or limited partnership is taxed like a sole proprietorship: The *business* isn't a taxpayer; the partners are. Partnerships, be they general or limited, don't pay taxes under any circumstances. A partnership files an "information" tax return that shows how much income or loss the partnership has allocated to the partners; the partners report that information on their personal tax returns. Consequently, businesses operated in partnership form are considered *conduits* for their partners. Just as with a sole proprietorship, if the partnership incurs losses during the year, the partners can use the losses allocated to them to offset other income they or their spouses have earned.

There's one great advantage in being taxed as a partnership: The partners are given almost completely free rein to allocate partnership profits and losses among themselves as they please by writing the allocations into the partnership agreement. Let's assume that Mr. Brown and Dr. White go into partnership to operate a restaurant. Mr. Brown will operate the restaurant; Dr. White, a successful surgeon bankrolling Mr. Brown, buys $50,000 in equipment to get the restaurant going. They agree that a fair division of the profits is one where 80 percent of the first $50,000 in profits goes to Mr. White (and 20 percent to Mr. Brown). After they've achieved $50,000, profits will be split fifty-fifty. They can accomplish this merely by writing it into the partnership agreement. What's even better is the ability to allocate losses. Dr. White, wealthy from his medical practice and in a high tax bracket, may be able to use the losses the restaurant business generates better than Mr. Brown, who is in a lower tax bracket. So they allocate 80 percent of the *losses* to Dr. White and 20 percent to Mr. Brown. It's even possible to allocate individual *items* of deduction to certain partners. For example, even though Mr. Brown and Dr. White decide to divide the profits equally, they're also free to decide that since Dr. White bought the equipment, all the depreciation deductions and investment tax credits will be allocated directly to Mr. Brown. In short, it's possible to write a partnership agreement custom-made for your needs, with the result that everyone is happy. Remember, however, that you can't have any "special" partnership tax allocations unless they're written into the partnership agreement.

The Tax Reform Act of 1986 placed a limitation on the ability of a partner to use tax losses allocated from a partnership. Let's return to the restaurant business in which Mr. Brown and Dr. White are partners. Dr. White is only an investor in the business; he doesn't work there. For the purposes of the Tax Reform Act, the restaurant is a "passive activity" to Dr. White. This means that if the restaurant partnership allocates any tax losses to Dr. White, he won't be able to use these losses to lower the taxes from his medical practice. He could use the losses from the restaurant to offset any income he might have from any other passive activity or from any income the restaurant earns in a future year.

There's one trap associated with partnership taxation you have to watch. Partners are taxed on partnership income that the partnership agreement *allocates* to them, *whether the income is distributed to them or not.* For example, let's say you're a one-third partner in a partnership that has net earnings of $300,000 during the year. Your partnership has a "managing partner" who's granted the right to determine whether to distribute the earnings or retain them for future expansion. You'll be taxed on one-third of $300,000, even though you haven't received the money and, what's far worse, don't have the cash to pay the tax. The problem is even more acute if you're a limited partner in a limited partnership: You'll always have a "managing partner" who makes all the decisions—the general partner.

"Regular" Corporations

When we turn to how a corporation is taxed, we turn to a completely different world. We began by seeing that when you operate your business in corporate form, the corporation earns income, not the owners. Consequently, the corporation, not the owners, pays taxes on the profits, and if there're no profits, the corporation owns the losses. Not only is the corporation a separate taxpayer, but corporations pay income taxes at different (generally *higher*) rates than do individuals. Accordingly, if and when the corporation distributes its earnings to its shareholders, the shareholders are taxed on the distributions (i.e., the *dividends*) at their individual rates. In other words, one of the things inherent in doing business in corporate form is the problem of *double taxation*. Stated more succinctly, the problem is one of getting money out of your corporation without paying taxes twice.

The best way to accomplish this is to make sure that whichever way you take money out, you don't take it out as a dividend, which is not deductible by the corporation. If the shareholders pay themselves salaries, which the corporation can deduct, the corporation won't pay taxes but the shareholders will. In such a situation the shareholders are indistinguishable from sole proprietors: The business doesn't pay any taxes; the shareholders do. If the shareholders can find some property to *rent* to their corporation, they'll achieve the same result: The corporation will receive a deduction when it pays the rent to the shareholders, and the shareholders will be taxed on the rental income.

Another way to avoid the problem of double taxation is to simply leave the earnings in the corporation, to the extent you can afford it. Unlike partners in a partnership, shareholders are taxed only on corporate earnings if and when they receive them. Until you receive the distribution, you can't be taxed. Why leave the money in the corporation? The corporation can use the retained earnings for expansion, or you can wait until another year to distribute the earnings, when your tax situation is more favorable. There's a tax risk, however, in leaving too much money in the corporation. If a corporation leaves more than $250,000 in earnings in the corporation ($150,000 for certain professional service corporations, such as accounting firms), the corporation can be subject to an *accumulated earnings tax,* a penalty designed to force corporations to distribute earnings. Despite this, even if you go over $250,000, you won't be subject to the accumulated earnings tax if you can prove to the IRS you have a valid business reason for retaining the earnings, such as saving for expansion.

Another way to avoid double taxation, if at least temporarily, is to have the shareholders *borrow* funds from their corporation. Since a loan isn't a dividend or compensation, the shareholder isn't taxed on the proceeds but still has the use of the money. This is only a temporary benefit, however, since the loan will have to be either repaid or canceled. If the loan is canceled, it's taxable income to the shareholder, just as if the shareholder had received the money from the corporation to pay the debt. Also, a recent change in the tax law requires that the loan be evidenced by a promissory note and bear a market rate of interest. If the interest rate the shareholder is required to pay to the corporation is below market, the difference will be considered taxable income to the shareholder.

A limitation inherent in operating as a regular corporation is that if the corporation *loses* money in any year, the shareholders cannot avail themselves of the losses on their personal returns, since the corporation is a separate taxpayer. The best the share-holders can do is hope that the corporation earns income in a future year and carry over the losses from the earlier year so as to lower the corporation's taxes in that year.

Thus far, it doesn't sound as if there're any tax advantages to operating a business as a regular corporation. There are, but it requires careful *planning* to attain the benefits. Here are some of them:

1. *Ability to "time" income.* We said that if a sole proprietor earns income at any time during the year, it's taxed to the sole proprietor. A partner is taxed on any income allocated to the partner, whether received or not. Sole proprietors and partners have no ability to time the receipt of income, and the resulting tax liability. But the owners of corporations do have this ability: They are taxed on income only when they receive it, either as dividends, compensation, rents, and the like. Why would a shareholder want to delay the receipt of income? The shareholder may foresee that in a later year he or she will be in a lower tax bracket than this year, because of retirement, semiretirement, lower earnings, or whatever.

Not only can a shareholder in a corporation defer income, but a shareholder can defer the income (and the tax) to himself while accelerating the deductions to the corporation. Unlike a sole proprietorship or a partnership, a corporation can, and should, adopt a *fiscal year* that ends on a date different from the December 31 year-end of all individuals. Let's assume that a corporation has a fiscal year (which is also its tax year) beginning on February 1 and ending on January 31 of each year. Let's further assume that the corporation pays salaries to its shareholders on January 15, 1986, zeroing out its earnings. The corporation will receive a *deduction* for the compensation paid for its year ending fifteen days later, on January 31, 1986. The shareholders, however, will have received the income in their individual tax year, which ends on December 31, 1986, and won't be liable for the tax until April 15, 1987 at the earliest. We can diagram this technique as follows:

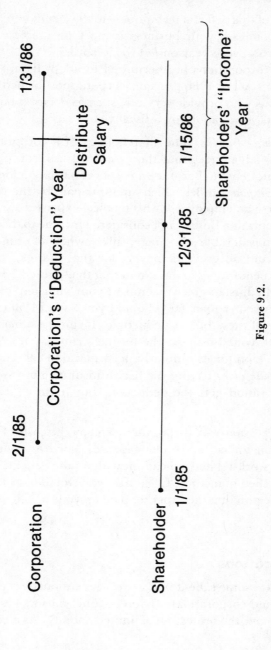

Figure 9.2.

As a result of this deferral technique—to the extent you can wait to receive income—if your business is more profitable every year, you pay taxes every year on *last year's income!*

Not all corporations are permitted to adopt fiscal years. The Tax Reform Act of 1986 prevents corporations formed by certain professionals who provide services, such as doctors, lawyers, and accountants, from adopting a fiscal year.

2. *Employee Benefits.* The shareholders of a corporation enjoy certain tax advantages that the owners of unincorporated businesses do not enjoy. For one, a corporation may adopt a *medical reimbursement plan,* under which amounts paid by the corporation to reimburse an employee for his medical expenses are deductible by the corporation but are not considered income to the employee. This is a considerable advantage, since owners of unincorporated business, and all other taxpayers for that matter, may deduct medical expenses only to the extent that they exceed 7.5 percent of the annual adjusted gross income. If your adjusted gross income for a given year equals $60,000 and you have $4,500 in medical bills, none of these bills is deductible. If, on the other hand, you incorporate your business, the business can pay the $4,500 and get a deduction for it. Similarly, a corporation can adopt an *accident and health plan,* paying the health insurance of its employees. The corporation gets the deduction, but it isn't income to the employees.

3. *Other Expenses.* A corporation can pay the costs of and obtain a deduction for certain other expenses, such as company cars, trips, and work-related education, without the benefits necessarily being included in income. Of course, you would have to be able to support a claim that the expenses paid on your behalf was business related.

S Corporations

Let's review some salient points we've mentioned regarding partnerships and corporations. If you conduct business as a corporation, you have the protection of limited liability. As a general partner in a partnership, you're exposed to liabilities caused by yourself, your partners, and your employees. But if you incorporate and lose money in your first year or years of operations, there's nothing you can do with the tax losses; you don't have the advantage inherent in a partnership or sole proprietorship of being able to pass tax losses directly through to yourself. So if you decide to start a business you're caught between a rock and hard place, giving up tax advantages for security or vice versa.

In acknowledgment of this problem, Congress in 1957 passed Subchapter S of the tax code. Under Subchapter S certain (but not all) corporations are permitted to elect *not* to be taxed as corporations but be taxed like sole proprietors and partners in partnerships. This means that for *tax purposes only* the existence of the corporation is ignored. If you elect Subchapter S status (and become an S corporation), you still have the same limited liability as a regular corporation (assuming you maintain all the corporate formalities so that no one can pierce the corporate veil), but you're taxed almost exactly like a partnership. If you're a 25 percent shareholder in an S corporation and the corporation loses $100,000 in its first year of operation, you're allocated $25,000 of the losses, which you can use to offset any other income you might have on your personal return (assuming that the S corporation is not a passive activity to you). The same is true, of course, of income. If you're a 25 percent shareholder, 25 percent of the income is allocated to you.

S corporation taxation is almost, but not quite, identical to the taxation of a partnership. Unlike a partnership, you don't have quite the flexibility to allocate profits and losses and particular items of deduction to given shareholders as you have in a partnership. You're limited to allocating profits and losses in accordance with the respective holdings of the shareholders.

S corporation treatment is designed only for small operating businesses. If you have more than thirty-five shareholders or if any one of your shareholders is itself a corporation, you won't qualify.

The planning technique many small businesses used to employ was to elect S corporation status for the initial year or years, when they expected to have net losses they would pass through to their shareholders. Later, when they did become profitable, they terminated their S corporation election. But that was before the Tax Reform Act of 1986, which made the corporate tax rates higher than individual tax rates. Now many businesses are electing S corporation status and retaining that status. They get the best of both worlds: a single tax and unlimited liability.

You may elect S corporation status by filing Form 2553 (pages 154–155) with the same IRS Service Center to which you would send your corporate tax return, which for an S corporation is Form 1120S. Form 1120S is an information return since an S corporation does not (with some exceptions) pay taxes. To qualify for S corporation status for any tax year, you must file Form 2553 within the first 2½ months of the tax year. If you don't, the election will be deemed an election for the next tax year. To elect, both the electing corporation and *all* its shareholders must consent. Not only that, but anyone who was a shareholder at any time during the first 2½ months of the year must consent, even if that person is no longer a shareholder on the day the election is filed.

The tax year of an S corporation is the calendar year (January 1 to December 31) unless you can prove to the IRS there's a valid business purpose for any other tax year.

The principal disadvantage of S corporation status is the thirty-five shareholders limitation. This limitation effectively limits the ability of an S corporation to raise capital. Since all shareholders must be individuals, it makes investment by venture capitalists impossible and eliminates the possibility that the corporation can become a public corporation while still an S corporation. It puts S corporations where they were meant to be: as vehicles for small businesses to retain limited liability while having their shareholders taxed directly.

ABILITY TO RAISE CAPITAL

Your ability to raise money will depend primarily on how successful your business is and how successful you can convince others it will become, regardless of the form of business you choose. But there're certain differences inherent in the form of business you choose.

As a sole proprietor, your ability to raise capital is limited to your ability to borrow money. There're no interests in your business you can peel off and sell to others, since your business is *you*. As a partner in a general partnership, you can raise money by selling partnership interests, but other than that you're limited to the ability of the partners to borrow money. Your ability to bring in new partners is limited by the fact that each general partner has unlimited liability.

Once your business is incorporated, you've a *theoretical* advantage over businesses that aren't. By selling shares to outsiders, you in effect sell pieces of your business. The outsiders may buy in the hope they'll receive dividends on their stock or, if the business really takes off, that it will become a public company, with the shares traded on a stock exchange. The advantage is theoretical since most companies don't pay dividends and never go public. Most people know that and are unwilling to invest in a close corporation.

If you conduct your business as a corporation, you may be successful in raising capital from a *venture capital* firm. A venture capital firm is a fund that invests in other businesses. It makes money when the business in which it invests is either bought by a larger firm at a high premium or goes public. For this reason, venture capitalists invest in smaller, start-up or developing businesses with a potential for growth; they don't usually invest in more mature, established companies or industries. Venture capital is a big business and it's growing: In 1986 alone, according to *Venture Capital Journal,* 587 venture capital firms raised $4.5 billion.

Not all businesses are candidates for venture capital. The ones that are generally are businesses that can show they can turn the venture capitalists' investment into immediate revenues and profits. High-tech firms make ideal venture capital candidates for just that reason. Also, a business isn't likely to generate interest from a venture capitalist if the business can be duplicated by oth-

Form **2553** (Rev. February 1987) Department of the Treasury Internal Revenue Service	**Election by a Small Business Corporation** (Under section 1362 of the Internal Revenue Code) ► For Paperwork Reduction Act Notice, see page 1 of Instructions. ► See separate instructions.	OMB No. 1545-0146 Expires 1-31-89

Note: *This election, to be treated as an "S corporation," can be approved only if all the tests in Instruction B are met.*

Part I   **Election Information**

Name of corporation (see instructions)	Employer identification number (see instructions)	Principal business activity and principal product or service (see instructions)
Number and street		Election is to be effective for tax year beginning (month, day, year)
City or town, state and ZIP code		Number of shares issued and outstanding (see instructions)

Is the corporation the outgrowth or continuation of any form of predecessor? . . . . ☐ Yes   ☐ No | Date and place of incorporation

If "Yes," state name of predecessor, type of organization, and period of its existence ► . . . .

A   If this election takes effect for the first tax year the corporation exists, enter the earliest of the following: (1) date the corporation first had shareholders,
(2) date the corporation first had assets, or (3) date the corporation began doing business. _____

B   Selected tax year: Annual return will be filed for tax year ending (month and day) ► . . . .
See instructions before entering your tax year. If the tax year ends any date other than December 31, you must complete Part II or Part IV on back. You
may want to complete Part III to make a back-up request.

C Name of each shareholder, person having a community property interest in the corporation's stock, and each tenant in common, joint tenant, and tenant by the entirety. (A husband and wife (and their estates) are counted as one shareholder in determining the number of shareholders without regard to the manner in which the stock is owned.)	**D** Shareholders' Consent Statement. We, the undersigned shareholders, consent to the corporation's election to be treated as an "S corporation" under section 1362(a). (Shareholders sign and date below.)*	**E** Stock owned		**F** Social security number (employer identification number for estates or trust)	**G** Tax year ends (month and day)
		Number of shares	Dates acquired		

*For this election to be valid, the consent of each shareholder, person having a community property interest in the corporation's stock, and each tenant in common, joint tenant, and tenant by the entirety must either appear above or be attached to this form. (See instructions for Column D, if continuation sheet or a separate consent statement is needed.)

Under penalties of perjury, I declare that I have examined this election, including accompanying schedules, and statements, and to the best of my knowledge and belief, it is true, correct, and complete.

Signature and
Title of Officer ►   Date ►

See Parts II, III, and IV on back.   Form **2553** (Rev 2-87)

Figure 9.3.

Part II   Selection of Tax Year Under Revenue Procedure 83-25 ＊

H   Check the applicable box below to indicate whether the corporation is:
☐ Adopting the tax year entered in item 8, Part I.
☐ Retaining the tax year entered in item 8, Part I.
☐ Changing to the tax year entered in item 8, Part I.

I   Check the applicable box below to indicate the representation statement the corporation is making as required under section 7.01 (item 4) of Revenue Procedure 83-25, 1983-1 C.B. 689 (or comparable section of the Revenue Procedure to be issued in 1987).

☐ Under penalties of perjury, I represent that shareholders holding more than half of the shares of the stock (as of the first day of the tax year to which the request relates) of the corporation have the same tax year or are concurrently changing to the tax year that the corporation adopts, retains, or changes to per item 8, Part I.

☐ Under penalties of perjury, I represent that the corporation is adopting, retaining, or changing to a tax year that coincides with its natural business year as verified by its satisfaction of the requirements of section 4.042(a), (b), (c), and (d) of Revenue Procedure 83-25 (or comparable section of the Revenue Procedure to be issued in 1987).

J   Check here ☐ if the tax year entered in item 8, Part I, is requested under the provisions of section 8 of Revenue Procedure 83-25 (or comparable section of the Revenue Procedure to be issued in 1987). Attach to Form 2553 a statement and other necessary information pursuant to the ruling request requirements of Revenue Procedure 87-1. The statement must include the business purpose for the desired tax year. See instructions.

＊At the time the Form 2553 and Instructions were printed, Revenue Procedure 83-25 was in the process of being revised.

Part III   Back-Up Request by Certain Corporations Initially Selecting a Fiscal Year (See Instructions.)

Check here ☐ if the corporation agrees to adopt or to change to a tax year ending December 31 if necessary for IRS to accept this election for S corporation status (temporary regulations section 18.1378-1(b)(2)(ii)(A)). This back-up request does not apply if the fiscal tax year request is approved by IRS or if the election to be an S corporation is not accepted.

Part IV   Request by Corporation for Tax Year Determination by IRS (See Instructions.)

Check here ☐ if the corporation requests the IRS to determine the permitted tax year for the corporation based on information submitted in Part I (and attached schedules). This request is made under provisions of temporary regulations section 18.1378-1(d).

☆ U.S. Government Printing Office: 1987—191-447/40063

Figure 9.3 (continued).

ers, once the product or service is proven. This means that companies whose success is based on trade secrets or patents are more likely to attract money than those that aren't.

Dealing with a venture capitalist doesn't represent free money; you'll have to give something up. Of course, you'll give up stock in your company, diluting your own interest. You'll probably also have to appoint a representative of the venture capital firm to sit on your board of directors. Depending on the deal you cut, you may find that you're restricted as to the salary or other benefits you can pay yourself while the venture capitalist holds some of your stock.

You might think that since the venture capitalists are armed with the money they have all the leverage when it comes to negotiating a deal. This isn't necessarily the case. There're lots of venture capital firms, and if you own a company that's ready to take off, you may find that a swarm of firms will be willing to deal with you. And some venture capitalists have more than money to offer; they have expertise in your business as well. That means sorting through the firms to determine which ones do have this experience. One that has may be able to assist you in a myriad of ways once you receive the funding and start growing.

The limited partnership is by far the best vehicle for raising capital. Because of this, thousands of apartment buildings, oil wells, and other "syndicated" properties are owned by limited partnerships, each having a few to many thousands of limited partners. As a limited partner you not only attain the limited liability you get as a shareholder in a corporation, but you can have certain tax benefits allocated directly to you. Even if the limited partnership never turns a profit, you may still come out ahead, or at least derive some benefit from the tax deductions you receive. Any business capable of generating deductions for investors can be operated as a limited partnership. If the business owns a fair number of capital assets eligible for depreciation deductions, the operators of the business (who usually act as the general partner) are often willing to trade the tax benefits for cash investments. Everyone is happy: The operators get the seed capital necessary to start or expand the business, and the investors receive a tax break and the opportunity to share in the profits of the business, all without any potential liability except for what they have invested.

Let's summarize. Easy as it is to start a sole proprietorship or a general partnership, it's very difficult to raise any capital once you have done so and, what's worse, you face the prospect of unlimited liability. If your business loses money, you'll be able to use the tax losses, but you'd be able to use the tax losses as a corporation electing to be taxed as an S corporation, unless the partnership or corporation is a passive activity to you. From the standpoint of raising capital, the limited partnership is best but difficult to operate. On the theory that a picture is worth a thousand words, the following is provided.

	Ease of Operation	Management and Control	Transfer-ability of Ownership Interest	Liability for Debts	Taxation	Ability to Raise Capital
Sole proprietorship	Excellent	Excellent	None	Unlimited	Poor	Poor
General partnership	Excellent	Poor	Limited	Unlimited	Good	Poor
Limited partnership	Poor	Excellent	Good	Unlimited for Gen.; Limited for others	Good	Excellent
Regular corporation	Good	Excellent	Good	Limited	Fair	Good
S corporation	Good	Excellent	Good	Limited	Good	Good

What form of doing business will you choose? There's no ready rule of thumb. But here's a prediction: If your business is successful, *eventually* you'll feel the need to incorporate. Incorporating your business and electing S corporation tax status may be the smart way to go. Consult with your accountant. By starting as a corporation you may prevent having to switch over if the fates should smile on your business.

Chapter **10**

PREPARING TO BUY: FINDING THE MONEY (OR "HOW TO DEAL WITH BANKERS")

It's not likely the seller is going to carry you for the full extent of the purchase price. Most likely you'll need to come up with some cash in order to buy the business. If you don't have all the cash you'll need at your fingertips, you'll have to borrow the money. If you're really lucky, you'll find a relative or friend willing to bankroll you. If you're like most people, you'll wind up talking to a banker.

BANKERS NEED YOU, TOO

Most people are intimidated by banks. After all, the largest buildings in most large cities are bank buildings. Banks radiate an (intended) aura of strength, solidity, and conservativeness. Why would any bank ever really *need* to deal with you?

Well, they do, and as banking has to compete to an ever greater extent with other types of financial institutions and types of investments (such as brokerage firms offering their own savings vehicles), your friendly neighborhood bank may need you more and more. Banks can make money only by lending money; the fewer good loans they make, the less they earn. That's why they advertise loans; they need your business.

Some banks, however, want your business more than others.

Though they won't admit it in these competitive times, banks specialize, both as to the type and size of loan business they do. Some banks are comfortable making loans to businesses; others specialize in home and car loans. The banks that do make loans to businesses tend to lend only to certain-size businesses. The biggest banks located in the downtown financial centers of major cities may be less likely to consider lending to a small business. Conversely, many small banks don't have the resources or sophistication to handle large loans.

The key, therefore, is to find the bank that's right for you. The right bank isn't the one that will provide you only with the funds to buy the business. The right bank is the one that will also work with you as you continue in business. This means shopping around. You should shop around for money in the same way you would for a house or a car. The banker you wind up dealing with should be interested in your business, not just in getting repaid. Once you're in business, a good banker can be a valuable part of your team, together with your lawyer and accountant.

As with cars and houses, the price of money will vary from bank to bank. Even if the interest rates don't vary, the "points," loan origination fees, and other charges will. Most important, the security interest banks require will differ from bank to bank. One bank may be willing to release part of the security when part of the loan has been repaid; another may insist on tying up all of the security until the entire loan is paid. One bank may require that personal assets (such as your house) also secure the loan; another may not. Remember: They want your business. *You can negotiate with banks.*

HOW TO OBTAIN A LOAN

Don't let the aura banks radiate fool you. Banks own computers, but computers don't make lending decisions; people do. These people are only partly motivated by the figures they gather from financial statements. A large part of any lending decision is the subjective feel a banker develops for the borrower. If the borrower doesn't impress the banker, the borrower's financial statements won't. Don't be fooled by that ubiquitous banking term *the loan committee*. A loan committee isn't a group of expressionless men in gray pinstripes crunching numbers on their calculators. If your loan officer is excited by you, he or she will excite the loan committee. The trick, then, is to motivate the loan officer.

The first step is to look at the lending transaction through the banker's eyes. Your banker is eager to see you succeed, just as you are. But your banker's goal is narrower: The banker needs to get the loan repaid. He'll analyze the loan request from that standpoint. It's your job to convince the banker that not only will you succeed in business, but that the bank will get its money back.

There is, of course, no guarantee you'll get any loan. But unless you're prepared to present certain documents to the banker, there's a certainty you won't get the loan. At a minimum, you'll need the following statements.

1. *Business Financial Statements.* The banker will conduct an investigation of the business you're looking to buy that's similar to the investigation you'll conduct. He or she will need to see the balance sheet and income statement of the business for at least three years and may well insist on *interim* financial statements, that is, financial statements updated from the date of the last fiscal year-end to the end of the most recent month or fiscal quarter. The quality of the financial statements is very important to bankers. They give far greater credence to financial statements prepared by outside accountants than to those prepared in house. Financial statements prepared by *certified* public accountants carry more clout than those that aren't. If the financial statements look rather amateurish to you, they'll look worse to a banker. If they're bad enough, the banker may not bother to look further.

Give the banker some additional information that usually doesn't appear on the balance sheet. He'll want to know about the *aging* of the accounts receivable and payable. Also include a list of equipment and real estate, if any. The banker will be impressed if you provide this information even before you're asked for it.

2. *Personal Financial Statements.* You'll also have to provide a statement showing your *personal* net worth. It's very likely you'll

have to personally guarantee the payment of the loan. As a result, the banker will want to know if you have any assets that could be converted into cash should the business default on the loan. You'll probably also have to provide him with your most recent personal tax returns.

3. *The Business Plan.* So far all that you've given the banker is numbers. This alone won't get you a loan. The banker will want to know who you are, how competent you and the people around you are, and what you intend to do with the money once you get it. The way you answer all these questions, and more, is by preparing a written business plan.

The first thing your business plan should tell the banker is why you want to buy the business. Be specific. Show the banker you've done your homework. If you've conducted any kind of market research or product survey, describe what you've found. Describe any improvements or changes you'll make in the conduct of the business and what the expected results will be in terms of increased sales or reduced overhead.

Next, your business plan should tell the banker how much money you need and *exactly* what you plan to do with it. A vague notion that the loan proceeds will be applied to general working capital won't be enough to get you the loan.

The next section of the business plan should be our old friend the pro forma. A well done, thought-out pro forma can be the difference between getting and not getting the loan. The pro forma tells you how much you can afford to borrow; it also tells the banker how much he'll be able to lend. You'll really impress the banker if you give him a number of pro formas, each based on varying assumptions. If you've been careful and thoughtful in preparing the pro forma, it's reasonable to believe you'll be careful and thoughtful in the conduct of the business. That's the impression you're trying to convey.

One of the entries in your pro forma will be the salary you intend to take out of the business. If profits are low, don't factor in a high salary; the banker doesn't want to place the loan at risk so you can draw a high salary not warranted by the business's profits. But don't factor in a salary that's too low; it won't impress the banker. The banker knows you'll have to take a reasonable salary out of the business in order to live. If the salary you factor in is too low, the banker will know you'll take out more and become uneasy about the future of his loan.

The last section of the business plan should describe the new management. The banker will want to know not only who you are but what your background is. The banker also will want to know who the other people are, whether they're present employees who'll remain in the business or new people you plan to bring on board. If your background is entirely engineering, the banker will want to know if anyone in the company has any financial or accounting experience. If your background is entirely finance and you're buying a high-tech business, the banker will want to know who'll handle the technical end of it. If you have a good management team lined up, don't be bashful; let the banker see how strong you are.

Most bankers have seen hundreds of business plans. But they don't read all the business plans they see and don't consider all those they read. There are certain things that distinguish good business plans from poor ones.

A good business plan is *concise*. No business plan should be longer than twenty-five pages and most can do the job in half that. If your business plan is the size of *War and Peace,* it won't impress him; he probably hasn't read *War and Peace* either. Too many business plans give the banker far more than he needs to know. There's no need to become too philosophic and go easy on the hyperbole. The banker doesn't care about your commitment to the free enterprise system, your devotion to hard work, or your opinion regarding the nation's or your state's future (he's read all that before). Just tell the banker, in a few well-chosen words, what you want to do and how you plan to do it.

A good business plan is *realistic*. If you're contemplating increases in earnings, you should be able to support the reasons why you think sales will go up or costs will go down. Remember this: *No banker has ever seen a business plan that predicted deteriorating profits.* If your business plan predicts good things to come, you need to distinguish your business plan from all the other ones the banker sees. You'll really impress the banker if you identify problem areas ahead and how you plan to deal with them and overcome them.

If you don't think you can write a good business plan, your accountant or business broker may help you. Also, in most medium- and large-size cities you'll be able to find a consultant who specializes in the preparation of business plans. You should consider it; it's that important.

WHO GETS THE MONEY . . . AND WHO DOESN'T

It's a simple fact of life that bankers are more comfortable lending money to businesses that have fixed assets than they are to those that don't. This means that your chances of obtaining a loan are greater in a manufacturing or distributing business than they are for a service business. If the business has fixed assets, such as machinery, equipment, real estate, and/or inventory, the banker will have security for the loan. If the borrower defaults, the banker can at least attach the assets to get his loan repaid. The sad fact is that if you don't have any assets, you're not likely to get a loan *unless you're willing to pledge personal assets.*

If you have fixed assets to pledge and the banker is willing to make the loan, you should try to limit the security you grant. Don't be disappointed if the banker won't lend you an amount of money equal to the assets you have. The loan to equity ratio will never be 100 percent. If you have $100,000 in assets to pledge, you won't get a $100,000 loan. That's standard. But you might try preventing the banker from getting his hands on every conceivable asset. For example, you might try to avoid granting a security interest in your accounts receivable. We mentioned in Chapter 5 that certain businesses factor their accounts receivable, that is, sell their receivables to a factor at a discount for cash. You may want to do that one day. But you won't be able to factor your receivables if they've already been pledged to a bank. If you have fixed assets to pledge to the banker, try to avoid a pledge of your personal assets. If you can't, at least try to get these assets released when part of the debt has been repaid.

THE SMALL BUSINESS ADMINISTRATION – A LITTLE HELP FROM THE FEDS

The Small Business Administration (SBA) is an agency of the federal government designed to assist small businesses. It provides counseling and literature on a variety of topics for an entrepreneur who's either planning to enter a business or who's already in business.

You may have heard about someone who "got an SBA loan." The SBA used to lend money and may do so again. Regrettably, the SBA is no longer in the business of making direct loans to small businesses. Rather, the SBA *guarantees* the loans banks make. In other words, if you obtain an SBA-guaranteed loan from a bank and you default, the bank will get paid by the SBA. The SBA will then go after you for the money.

Will a bank lend you money on an SBA guarantee it otherwise wouldn't lend you? Probably not. The reason is that the SBA will guarantee no more than 90 percent of the loan, and often less. The bank will be on the hook for the rest if you default. A bank isn't likely to lend money to a bad credit risk or to a business with no security even if they stand to lose only 10 percent or 20 percent of the money. Also, if the bank won't lend you any money, the SBA probably won't guarantee the loan in the first place.

There are, however, advantages in SBA-guaranteed loans. For one, the SBA places a ceiling on the rate of interest the bank can charge. If your loan is guaranteed by the SBA, you'll save a point or two in interest. Also, a bank will lend money for a longer term if the loan is guaranteed by the SBA. Generally, banks won't lend money for a period more than four or five years. With an SBA guarantee, you can stretch the period out to six or seven years.

Getting the SBA to guarantee a loan is no easier than getting the loan from the bank. The SBA will want to see the same pro formas and financial statements the banker will. The SBA will scrutinize carefully the amount of money you'll take out of the business in salary. After all, it's taxpayers' money they're dealing with, and they don't want to place taxpayers' money at risk so you can draw a high salary.

The procedure for getting an SBA-guaranteed loan doesn't differ greatly from a nonguaranteed loan. Start out by dealing with your banker, not the SBA. If your banker doesn't deal with the SBA, you might consider dealing with another banker. If your banker does, he'll direct you to the SBA at the proper time.

Chapter **11**

STEP BY STEP TO CLOSING

Let's assume the best: After a few weeks of negotiation between you and Mr. Houston, you and he have come to a tentative understanding. You're going to buy the assets of Houston Sash & Door for $1,200,000, payable $200,000 in cash at the closing and $1,000,000 with your $1,000,000 promissory note. The note will bear interest at the rate of 10 percent per year and is payable, principal and interest, every month for seven years. Each monthly payment amounts to $16,601.20. Payment of the note is secured by the fixed assets, inventory, and accounts receivable of the business. For the sake of simplicity, we'll assume that no separate amount will be paid for a consulting agreement or a noncompetition agreement. We'll also assume that you'll purchase the assets yourself; no corporation will be formed to purchase the assets.

THE LETTER OF INTENT

The first step in any well-structured purchase is the letter of intent. Take a look at the sample letter of intent in Appendix 1 (pages 191–193).

The first thing that should be apparent to you from reading it is that it's *not legally binding*. Even after the seller accepts the letter of intent by signing it, the seller is not legally bound to sell and the buyer is not legally bound to buy. Despite the fact it isn't binding, the letter of intent accomplishes a few important things. It reduces to writing the major terms of the sale, such as the price, the terms of the promissory note, and the *form* of the sale, that is, whether the owner's stock or the business's assets are being bought. The letter of intent also makes clear all the things that will have to be accomplished before you'll sign the purchase agreement, which after it's signed *will* obligate you to buy the business. In addition, the letter of intent grants you permission to contact the seller's lawyer, accountant, and banker, so you can get your investigation rolling.

There're two provisions in the letter of intent that are legally binding. The buyer obligates himself or herself not to disclose to anyone (other than to the people the seller authorizes) that there are negotiations being conducted for the sale of the business or anything else about the seller's business the buyer learns. Of course, the buyer will be free to disclose anything should he buy the business. This provision protects the seller if the sale doesn't close. The second legally binding provision prevents the seller from shopping the letter of intent, that is, going to others in the hope of getting a better deal. If negotiations don't break down within the ninety-day period that both sides have in which to close, the seller can't deal with anyone else.

A well-drafted letter of intent prevents either side from going too fast or too slow. The seller learns you're serious about buying but that you've got a lot to do before you can close the deal. The buyer realizes he can't delay; if he takes too long, the seller will be free to sell to others.

The letter of intent also serves to show others that the buyer and seller are serious. It's better to go to the seller's landlord in the hope of negotiating a new lease and say "I've just executed a letter of intent with Mr. Houston for the purchase of Houston Sash & Door" than have to say "I'm thinking about buying Houston Sash & Door."

You need to be careful when drafting a letter of intent. It's possible to enter into a binding contract without realizing it. Because of this, the letter of intent should state that, except as otherwise specifically noted, it is *not* designed to obligate either side to close the sale.

START YOUR INVESTIGATION

Once you've obtained the seller's signature on the letter of intent, the real work begins. Your accountant should begin analyzing the financial statements and other records of the seller's business. Your attorney should begin the legal investigation, which includes checking the records of the secretary of state for any UCC-1 filings against the seller's fixed assets and the records of the county clerk for any liens against real estate. If the seller has already told you there're lawsuits involving the business, your attorney should review them. If the sale involves the seller's stock rather than the assets, your attorney should review the articles of incorporation, by-laws, corporate minutes, and stock transfer ledger of the corporation. You should start preparing a pro forma. To the extent you're permitted by the letter of intent, you should visit the seller's banker, landlord, customers, and suppliers. Your attorney should contact the seller's attorney. At this stage you should take the position that you've not decided whether to buy; your investigation should be to determine whether you ultimately want to buy and whether the price and terms indicated in the letter of intent are appropriate.

THE PURCHASE AGREEMENT

There may be no document you'll ever sign in your life that's as important as the purchase agreement for the purchase of a business. You may have to live with whatever is (or isn't!) in that agreement for a very long time. Its contents may affect your financial security. So it needs to be drafted with care.

The purchase agreement should be drafted by the *buyer's* attorney. An attorney conversant with the issues surrounding the purchase of any business can make a purchase agreement more advantageous to his client, the buyer, by adding a few key phrases here, dropping a few words there. An agreement that is grossly one-sided usually winds up being a waste of time and money since it won't be accepted. But an agreement that appears to be even-handed may have a ringer or two that even an astute attorney won't catch. We'll see some examples of this shortly.

Scan the sample purchase agreement that starts on page 196 (Appendix 2). It's been drafted from the buyer's point of view. The seller's attorney may have a few things to say about it. The numbers in the margin correspond to the numbered paragraphs below.

1. We said in Chapter 6 that if you buy the assets directly from the corporation, the owners of the corporation don't need to be a party to the agreement. Why is Mr. Houston a party to this agreement? Though he doesn't have to be, the buyer should want him included. In Section 7 the seller will make certain "representations and warranties" to the buyer. If these representations and warranties aren't fulfilled, the buyer may have to sue. But we don't want to sue just a corporation, which may since have been dissolved. We want the individual on the hook as well.

2. The seller is going to have to list every item being sold in an exhibit that will accompany the agreement. This prevents the buyer from thinking that all the assets *used* in the business are being sold. As we saw in Chapter 3, some of the assets a business uses may not be *owned* by the business.

3. The buyer is going to pay for only those liabilities he knows about. It's one of the big advantages inherent in buying assets, as opposed to buying the owner's stock. We say the same thing in Section 3 of the agreement.

4. The terms of the promissory note usually won't appear in the agreement. Instead, the note itself will have been prepared and attached to the agreement.

5. The promissory note will be secured by a security agreement, which the buyer will sign at the closing. The buyer will also sign a UCC-1 financing statement, which the seller's attorney will

file with the secretary of state or county clerk after the closing. The UCC-1 financing statement provides notice to anyone else who might want to loan funds to the buyer that the seller's rights in the secured assets come first.

6. If the seller wants the buyer to assume and pay for a liability or take over a contractual obligation, it must be listed in either Exhibit 5 or Exhibit 6. Presumably, the seller will attempt to list every liability he or she is aware of, since the buyer won't be bound by any which aren't listed.

7. Section 3.1 is a holdback provision. If the buyer winds up having to pay a debt the seller didn't disclose in Exhibits 5 or 6, the buyer will be able to deduct the amount paid from the amount held back at the closing. In this holdback clause the buyer's attorney is appointed as the *escrow agent*. Many sellers won't agree to this type of arrangement and will insist that an independent escrow agent be appointed. The amount held back, $10,000, is also subject to negotiation. Obviously a buyer will want more held back, and the seller less. The letter that accompanies the purchase agreement will spell out the length of time the money is held back and the "rules" governing when the escrow agent can take money out to pay a bill.

8. Section 4 represents the allocation of the purchase price to the various assets bought. As we saw in Chapter 6, buyer and seller are likely to be on opposite sides of the fence with respect to each item, since what's a tax advantage for the buyer may hurt the seller and vice versa. Note that the price assigned to the land has been broken out from the price assigned to the building that sits on it. The building is depreciable; the land isn't. An allocation for "agreement not to compete" is included, even though we don't have one in our agreement. If we had, the amount to be paid for the agreement would be spelled out in the agreement itself and listed in this section.

9. Once you sign the purchase agreement, you're obligated to go through with the deal. If the seller refuses to turn over the business on the scheduled date of closing, you can sue the seller. The

seller can sue you if you fail to deliver the required funds on the closing date. However, if an obligation a party is required to fulfill in the agreement hasn't been met by the scheduled date, the closing can be postponed. If the closing hasn't occurred by April 30, 1988, each party is free to go his or her separate way.

10. Since you're buying the assets instead of the corporate stock, you're not interested in the corporation's minute books and stock ledger records. You'd be very interested in these items if you were buying the corporation itself. If so, the seller wouldn't need to sign a bill of sale for the assets, since the assets themselves would not be sold. But there're certain *other* things the seller would have to sign at the closing. Since the owner would likely be the president and a director of the corporation being sold, you'd want him and all his other officers and directors to deliver their *resignations* at the closing. Immediately after the closing, you'd conduct your first shareholders' and directors' meeting, electing new directors and officers.

11. There may be no section of the purchase agreement more important to the buyer than the seller's "representations and warranties." The seller may have fudged on a few items when negotiating the sale with you, but if the seller fudges on any representation or warranty, it's a breach of contract. If anything said turns out not to be true and winds up lowering the value of the business, you can hold back part of the money that hasn't yet been paid or sue to recover what has been paid. Sellers have the tendency to lose interest on any provision in the purchase agreement that follows the section that tells them how much money they're entitled to. That's a mistake.

12. The representation regarding the seller's *corporate standing* is less important when buying assets than when buying the corporation itself. You don't want to buy a corporation only to find out that the secretary of state dissolved the corporation three years back for failure to pay franchise taxes! (Your attorney will check this out prior to closing.)

13. On the theory that what you see is what you get, you don't want to find out later that the seller conducted part of his business through an entity you didn't buy.

14. The representation regarding "Transactions with Certain Persons" is designed to smoke out business dealings that aren't at arm's length. If a certain large customer is also controlled by the seller, you find that out here.

15. This is where you find out if there are any deferred compensation arrangements or employment agreements you weren't told about. Again, this is more important if you're buying the corporation itself.

16. The final sentence of Section 7(c) assures you that all the assets used by the business are owned by the business and that you won't have to buy replacement assets to keep the business going.

17. The representations contained in Section 7(d) assures you there isn't a loan agreement, lease, or another contract floating around that prevents the seller from selling the assets to you or won't cause some loan to come due if the assets are sold. The seller may not be aware of the fine print of his own loan agreements. This representation is no substitute for your review of all the seller's agreements.

18. In this paragraph the seller is promising that the financial statements are complete and correct. Note that the seller has had to provide *interim* financial statements, for the month ending just before the date of the purchase agreement.

19. It's important to know that not only have all the seller's taxes been paid but that there aren't any lurking problems with the tax collectors. If there's been an audit or if interest and penalties resulting from late filing may be due, you need to know this. Since you can't estimate how much tax may be owing as a result of an audit only recently conducted, the holdback provision assumes added importance.

20. You don't want to buy a lawsuit. In this section the seller is promising you he doesn't know of any.

21. Read Section 7(h) carefully. It represents an example of how a purposefully *omitted* phrase can change the meaning of a promise. The section says that the seller hasn't violated any existing or proposed laws, regulations, or rules. The section *doesn't* say the seller *isn't aware of* any violations of any existing laws, regulations, or rules. If Section 7(h) began with the phrase "To the best of seller's knowledge . . ." the meaning of this section would be changed completely. As it stands now, this section represents a *guarantee* on the part of the seller that there are no existing laws or rules that could affect the business being sold. If there's a law out there just passed that would adversely affect the business, the seller has breached the agreement, whether he knew of the law or not. This is a perfect example of the benefit in having the buyer's attorney write the agreement.

22. The seller becomes obligated in this section to provide you with a complete list of some very important items, such as contracts, leases, agreements with labor unions, pension and profit-sharing plans, and licenses. If any one of these is omitted, it's a breach of the agreement.

23. This is one you might have to explain to the seller. It's designed to smoke out any kickback given or any other illegal arrangement made but that you may not be comfortable continuing.

24. Section 8 is very important to a buyer. There may be a period of weeks or months between the signing of the purchase agreement and the closing. During the period the seller has little motivation to keep the business humming along. The motivation is provided in this section, which requires the seller to operate the business in the same manner as before. It prevents the seller from doing anything out of the ordinary course of business without telling you about it: The seller can't grant raises or bonuses, enter into binding contracts, or do anything else except to keep manufacturing and selling products.

25. After the purchase agreement is signed, you're going to want to keep in close touch with the day-to-day operations of the business. This section gives you that right.

26. Section 10 represents the buyer's escape clause. If any of the things mentioned in Section 10 occurs or, if required, fails to occur prior to the closing, the buyer doesn't have to go through with the sale. If the agreement is written by the buyer's attorney, the attorney will attempt to draft this provision as broadly as possible. The seller's attorney will attempt to narrow it. For example, the phrase "material adverse change" in paragraph (c) isn't defined. If the buyer gets cold feet, he or she will use any change in the business from the date of the agreement to avoid going through with the sale.

27. We covered in Chapter 6 the duties of the seller and the buyer under the bulk sales act. You won't need such a provision if the owner's stock, as opposed to the assets, are being purchased or if the assets being purchased don't include the bulk of the seller's inventory, if any. On occasion buyer and seller will waive compliance with the act, with the seller agreeing to pay any undisclosed debts. If this is the case, a section speaking to the *waiver of compliance* with the act should appear here.

28. Section 12 is vitally important to the buyer. It says, in effect, that the seller will reimburse the buyer for anything that turns out not to be true in the agreement. In other words, the buyer won't be limited to the money held back at the closing, but you can sue to recover any amount resulting from something undisclosed by the seller.

The phrase "jointly and severally" in the first sentence is an important bit of legalese. Let's assume that the seller doesn't tell you about a $50,000 bill owed to a supplier you're going to have to pay. Who's going to have to pay the $50,000 to you, Houston Sash & Door, Inc. or Mr. Houston? The phrase "jointly and severally" means you can sue either Houston Sash & Door or Mr. Houston himself *for the entire amount*. That's important, since the corporation may be liquidated or not have any funds after the sale.

29. Note that Mr. Houston will sign the agreement in two capacities. He'll sign as the president of the corporation and in his own individual capacity.

The purchase agreement looks like quite a mouthful, doesn't it? In practice, most purchase agreements are even more extensive! We've eliminated quite a bit of the legal jargon.

Every so often you'll encounter a seller who takes one look at a purchase agreement that's twenty pages long and gags. On occasion a seller will say to the buyer, in effect: "Look, I don't have anything to hide, and you've already seen everything there is to see. I can't be bothered with this type of stuff. Heck, I don't even understand half the lawyer talk that's in it. It only exists to pump up lawyers' fees anyway. Why don't I just write up the terms on one sheet of paper and we'll let it go at that?"

Don't do it! The purchase agreement exists for the principal benefit of the buyer, not the seller. Anyone can be a seller; all you need to do to be a seller is show up at the closing with an outstretched palm and wait for the money. If the seller isn't interested in taking the time to read and understand the purchase agreement, it's not likely he was interested in telling you everything you needed to learn about the business in the first place. Hang tough and insist that the purchase agreement be signed as your attorney prepared it.

THINGS TO DO PRIOR TO CLOSING

You're going to be awfully busy prior to closing. If you're going to form a corporation in order to buy the business, give your attorney plenty of time to form it. After you're sure the name under which you'll be operating is available (if your name will be different from the name under which the seller operates), you should start preparing business cards, stationery, and business forms. The idea is to hit the ground running, so that all you need to do once you take over the business is start selling.

If you haven't had the opportunity to visit all the seller's principal customers and suppliers prior to signing the purchase agreement, you should start doing so. You don't want any of these important people to be dealing with a stranger after you take over. If your seller has had problems with any supplier or customer, you may be able to improve the business even before you buy it. If a supplier has been dealing with the seller on a COD basis, you might convince the supplier a new day is dawning and that the supplier should grant you easier credit terms. Some suppliers grant better-paying customers discounts for fast payment. One or more of these suppliers may do the same for you. Certain customers may have stopped dealing with the seller because of slow service or the inferior quality of the goods shipped. You might convince these former, or soon to be former, customers to give the business another chance now that you're about to take over.

One of the first things you should do after you sign the purchase agreement is to meet with the key employees. By this time you should know who they are, their duties, and how much they get paid. This will be a time of great uncertainty for them; you'll want to allay their fears and anxieties about the future. They may have some pretty good ideas about changes that need to be made. They may also be aware, to an even greater extent than the owner, of some problem areas.

Your attorney will be busy too. He or she will be checking (if not prior to the signing of the purchase agreement) all the contracts, leases, and schedules provided by the seller, as required by the purchase agreement. Your attorney will also have the responsibility to prepare and send out to creditors the notices required under the bulk sales act.

If you weren't able to talk to the landlord prior to signing the purchase agreement, now's the time to do so. The threat you may not close the sale unless he grants you a new lease may be just the thing it takes to get him to do just that.

The purchase agreement should provide you with a list of all the assets and the inventory. No *earlier* than a day or two prior to the closing, visit the business and physically *count* the assets and the inventory. If the business stocks 50,000 record albums, you won't be able to count all of them, but you should still be able to sense whether the inventory has been depleted since you last saw it. You should not only identify the fixed assets, you should check to see that everything still works. If an important item is missing or has broken since you last saw it, the seller has breached the purchase agreement. This should result in a lower purchase price, to reflect the missing or broken item.

Shortly before the closing your attorney may wish to meet with the seller's attorney to conduct a *preclosing*. This is nothing more than an exchange and review of all the documents required to be signed at the closing. If there're any requirements that still need to be fulfilled by either party, these should be noted. For example, most purchase agreements require that the cash portion of the purchase price be paid in the form of a cashier's check or a certified check. Every now and then a buyer who forgets about this requirement shows up at the closing with his personal checkbook, expecting to buy a business with a personal check. Make sure you're prepared to do at the closing everything required of you.

The purchase agreement often will require that certain items, such as real estate taxes, personal property taxes, and utility charges, be *pro rated* as of the date of the closing. If this is the case, you should determine what the charges are or will be, so that the proper amounts can be charged to the buyer and seller at the closing. These items are usually small, and often the buyer will be permitted to bring a personal check to the closing to cover these amounts.

THE CLOSING

What happens at the closing itself? If the buyer and seller, and their respective attorneys, have done their jobs properly, not much! A few documents, such as the bill of sale, a consulting agreement and/or noncompetition agreement, the promissory note, the security agreement, and the UCC-1 financing statement, are signed. If the sale involves the sale of the owner's stock, share certificates will be endorsed and officers' and directors' resignations signed. And of course, the check for the purchase price is endorsed and handed over. No matter how complex a business is, if the respective parties have done their work prior to the closing, the closing itself shouldn't take more than an hour. If a closing takes eight hours, someone has screwed up.

The worst thing that can happen (and it happens) is for *negotiations* to take place at the closing. It usually occurs when one party hasn't bothered to read all the documents prior to the closing. At some point the seller, with nothing to do while somone else is getting coffee or photocopying documents, picks up a document, reads it for the first time, and says, "Say! What's this business about my indemnifying the buyer? I never agreed to that!" How's this possible? After all, the seller signed the purchase agreement. It happens because people don't always read what they sign, particularly if the print is small and the writing goes on forever and isn't in readable English anyway. When this occurs, one of the attorneys or the broker has screwed up.

POSTCLOSING MATTERS

When you leave the closing you own the business, but you're not quite done. Certain people will need to be notified you now own the business. You may need the seller's help in doing this. If you're moving the business, the post office, the telephone company, and the public utilities will have to be notified where to send the bills. If you're going to change the name of the business, these people will have to be notified.

Chapter **12**

SOME THOUGHTS ON SELLING A BUSINESS

The business you're now looking to buy may one day become the business you'll be looking to sell. The business that today looks like a once-in-a-lifetime opportunity may become the financial and psychological albatross you have to unload. With this in mind, let's devote some thought to selling a business.

A QUESTION OF TIMING: WHEN TO OFFER THE BUSINESS FOR SALE

One of my law partners keeps threatening to write a book titled *When Should You Pull the Plug?* It promises to be an important, albeit short, book. The answer to the question is "not too late." My partner wants to write this book out of the frustration of seeing too many business owners hang on for too long and, in many instances, having nothing left to sell once the decision to sell is made.

Too often a business owner allows devotion, optimism, inertia, or a combination of the three to deflect him or her from offering the business for sale until it's too late. In the interim a number of things occur that make matters worse. If the problem has been poor sales, sales may get worse, caused in part by the owner's short-timer's attitude. To keep the business afloat, owners will often borrow money, placing more debt on the business's assets, causing the value of the business to decline and even jeopardizing the business's retention of the assets. As the slide continues, owners attempt to cut costs, often eliminating muscle along with fat. The elimination of salespersons and advertising and public relations expenses may lower overhead, but it also inhibits the ability to generate sales. A large- or medium-sized business becomes a small business in the process.

Not all business's are sold because of poor financial condition. As we saw in Chapter 2, businesses are often sold for personal reasons, such as the illness, death, or impending retirement of the owner. If an owner is getting up in years and realizes he or she will want to retire, the time to start looking for a sale is before the retirement date is imminent. Even if the business is solid, the price will go down and/or the terms will be tougher if the buyer senses the seller is under a compulsion to sell.

Even if the business is in fine shape and you aren't planning on retiring, you may find you don't like the business and want out. A business broker I know has the best rule of thumb for when to start thinking of selling: when you no longer want to get out of bed in the morning.

HOW TO SELL: DEALING WITH BUSINESS BROKERS

Let's assume you've decided to sell your business. There're two basic methods to accomplish this: on your own or through a business broker.

If you decide to sell the business by yourself, you could run an ad in the "Business Opportunities" section of the local newspaper, notify the local chamber of commerce, or rely on word of mouth. The advantage in selling on your own is that you'll save on whatever commission you'd have incurred to the broker. But there're considerable disadvantages. Even if you run a blind ad in the newspaper, your employees, customers, or suppliers may well learn you're selling, with all the problems of customer relations and employee morale this entails. You'll also wind up dealing with a parade of prospective buyers, some who aren't interested and others who aren't qualified. Some may even be looking for some free advice. The time you take in weeding through all these "Lookie Lou's" is time away from your business.

Selling through a business broker will obviate these problems. The fact you're selling will be relatively confidential, limited to only those persons the broker prescreens. The broker will have described the business to the prospective buyer (often without identifying the business), informed the buyer of the asking price and terms, and determined whether the buyer can pay.

A good broker will also provide you with other valuable services. An experienced broker will be able to tell you what you can expect to receive for your business. If you think your business is worth $500,000 but the broker knows that similar businesses have sold for $150,000, the broker can tell you you're wasting your time trying to sell for $500,000. A good broker will help you structure the sale and minimize the risk that you'll be back in the business should the buyer default.

If and when you become serious about selling, the advice here is not to try to sell on your own. Your next consideration should be the choice of a broker and, once the broker is selected, the terms under which you'll deal with the broker.

Selecting the Right Broker

Some years back a real estate broker appeared in my office. He had just picked up a listing to sell a business, and it quickly became apparent to me that this realtor knew nothing about selling businesses. When I asked him whether the sale was going to be a stock sale or an asset sale, a blank look came over his face and he blurted out, "Both." This was not a person who was going to give his client any advice about all the advantages and disadvantages of stock sales versus asset sales, which we covered in Chapter 6, or any other good advice.

Choose a broker carefully. Your best bet is to select a broker who deals only in *business* brokerage. Two nationwide chains, VR Business Brokers and Corporate Investment International, specialize in business brokerage. But within each chain each office is locally owned, so the quality of brokers may vary wildly from city to city and even within each local office. In addition to these two chains, most large cities will have a fair number of independent business brokers.

Business brokers have a tendency to specialize. Some are comfortable with small businesses that sell in the $100,000 range. Others won't touch a business sells for under $500,000 or $1 million. It's important to inquire whether the broker you're dealing with has any experience selling a business in your range.

A few brokers restrict their brokerage to certain types of businesses. For example, certain brokers specialize in the sale of restaurants. The brokers who specialize are very knowledgeable about the price and terms a business could command and may even have an inventory of prospective buyers. If you can find a broker in your town who specializes in your business, that's the place to start.

Coming to Terms with the Broker

Any business broker with any sense will require you to sign an exclusive listing agreement. The agreement will specify that only that broker can sell the business during the period of the agreement (or even after the agreement expires if the broker introduces you to the buyer during the listing period). If you use another broker in violation of the agreement, you'll still have to pay the broker the required commission.

Try to arrange an agreement with the broker such that you don't owe the broker any commission if you sell the business to a person you find. For example, if you're lucky and your brother-in-law decides he wants to buy your business, you won't have to pay a commission. But if you don't write such a provision into the listing agreement, you'll have to pay a commission even if the broker had nothing to do with selling the business to your brother-in-law.

The duration of the listing agreement is important. No reputable broker will take a listing for less than three months; it's impossible to do a business justice in a shorter period of time. But you can get hurt with a listing that runs too long. If the broker turns out to be a dud, you're stuck with that broker until the listing runs out.

Depending on the size of the business, you should be able to negotiate the broker's commission. The *smaller* the business, the *higher* the percentage of the sales price that will go to the broker. Forget about the standard 6 or 7 percent you'd pay to a realtor if you were selling your home. For a business in the $100,000 range, the commission will be 10 to 12 percent. For larger businesses the commission will be less, often sliding downward pursuant to a *Lehman formula*. A typical Lehman formula will earn the broker 5 percent for the first $1 million, 4 percent for $1 million to $2 million, 3 percent for $2 million to $3 million, 2 percent for $3 million to $4 million, and 1 percent above $4 million. You can also negotiate a Lehman formula for smaller sales.

Most brokers will attempt to earn their commission at the time of sale, even if most of the purchase price is to be paid over a period of time. You should try to negotiate a commission that is due in part at closing with the balance payable as the purchase price is received.

PREPARING TO SELL

If you were preparing to sell your home, one of the first things you'd do is spruce it up. You'd make sure that when prospective buyers arrived, the yard was mowed and the kids' toys were stowed. You'd make sure that any needed touch-up painting or repairs were done as well. The same holds true if you're preparing to sell your business. The buyers are only human and will be turned off by a business that looks like a junkyard. Your business may not be a model of efficiency but at least you can give it that appearance.

Like the sale of your home, you should consider touching up the financial condition of your business. Reread Chapter 4; there we dealt at length with some of the things sellers do to prettify their financial statements. If your buyer isn't astute (and hasn't read this book), the buyer may not notice some of the things you did to pump up your sales, earnings, or current assets.

Even if your buyer is astute, there're a few things you might do to enhance your business. Let's assume that the business is being sued for a small amount. Whether or not the suit is frivolous, you might be better off settling the suit for a few hundred dollars than having to constantly explain what the suit is all about and driving off a considerable percentage of prospective buyers who fear any kind of litigation.

You could ease the sale by doing some spadework. Let's assume your lease is about to expire. Any intelligent buyer will be concerned about what the terms of the new lease will be. You could discreetly ask the landlord about these terms. It's better to be able to tell a prospective buyer "I'm reasonably certain you'll be able to sign a new lease at an increase of only 5 percent" than to leave the buyer guessing. The same holds true of supply contracts, insurance coverage, and the like. If you can find out in advance what the renewal terms will be, you'll make the buyer's job easier and facilitate a quicker sale.

QUALIFYING THE BUYER

How badly do you want to get out? If the answer is that under no circumstances do you ever want to get back into the business once you've left, you've got two choices: either sell the business for cash (which includes requiring the buyer to find his or her own financing so that you get paid in cash at closing) or make sure that any financing you provide the buyer will be paid. If you do neither of these, you'll be faced with the extremely unpleasant choice of forgetting about the debt or reentering the business.

If you sell the business for cash, you won't care how the business does after you've sold it. But if you leave the closing table with the buyer's promissory note, you'll have a vested interest in the buyer's ability either to run the business profitably or, if there are no profits, to pay the note out of the buyer's other assets.

If you have a good broker, the broker will determine whether the buyer is qualified, both in terms of ability and financial strength. Just as a buyer shouldn't fear being nosey about every aspect of your business, you shouldn't refrain from making serious inquiries into the buyer's abilities and finances. Find out if the buyer has ever run a business, and if so, how it fared. If the buyer has already taken a business or two into bankruptcy, yours may be next in line. Some people have a habit of success; others, the opposite.

Even if the buyer doesn't have a history of failure, the business may not be suitable for him. We saw earlier that a business that can be run easily and profitably by a couple may be unsuitable for a single person. A business that requires a strong-willed individual, ready and willing to kick a few behinds, may be unsuited for a mild-mannered widow. If you finance the buyer and the buyer makes a mistake, it's your mistake.

It isn't enough that the buyer has just enough cash to make the down payment. The buyer should have sufficient capital to survive a downturn, especially the initial downturn that may result from the buyer learning the ropes. Again, a good business broker will advise the buyer as to the total capital needed to start the business, which is invariably more than the purchase price.

Here's a real horror to avoid: A certain percentage of "buyers" are con artists. Their scam is to tell a good story, get into a good business at little or no money down, quickly sell off the receivables and equipment at a deep discount, and slip away into the night, leaving the seller with a ruined business and a worthless promissory note. Very often the seller finds that "buyer" was using a fictitious name! By that time the "buyer" is in a different city under a different name working on his next victim. Years of effort go down the drain because the seller wasn't careful about checking out the "buyer."

Even if the buyer isn't an out-and-out crook, the effect can be the same when dealing with an incompetent buyer. Unfortunately there're a growing number of people who've graduated from no-money-down seminars who think they can leverage themselves into riches. If you sell to one of these people and finance him, his rude awakening that it can't be done becomes your loss.

NEGOTIATING THE SALE

Let's repeat here some earlier advice: negotiate in secret. Don't let your customers, suppliers, and employees find out a transfer is in the offing.

If you're determined you never want to think about this business again and certainly don't ever want to reenter it, you should try to hold out for an all-cash sale. If you do, you'll undoubtedly have to accept a lower sales price. But even if you sell the business for cash, it doesn't mean you're out for good. Along the line you may have personally guaranteed some of the business's debts or pledged your personal assets to secure these debts. Even if the buyer agrees to assume these debts, the buyer's assumption doesn't get you off the hook. You should attempt to get the lender's consent to replace your personal guarantee with your buyer's. If the lender refuses (and the lender may well refuse; the buyer's credit may not be as good as yours), you should demand that the loans you've personally guaranteed be paid *at closing*. You should go so far as to require that checks be issued to the lender at closing, with the lender returning the promissory note to you marked "Paid." Failing to do so could result in an unexpected disaster should the buyer default on the note.

Most of the legalese in the purchase agreement benefits the buyer, not the seller. After all, it's the buyer, who wasn't there while the seller was running the business, who needs to be protected. Most of the representations and warranties (see Section 7 of the purchase agreement) run in favor of the buyer. But there's one aspect of the deal the seller must structure with great care: the security that stands behind the promissory note. If the note isn't paid, you can sue the buyer. But if the buyer can't pay on the note, winning a judgment against the buyer probably won't do you any good. If the buyer goes into bankruptcy, you won't even be allowed to sue. The security you receive is your assurance you'll be able to get at least something if the note isn't paid. You need to be careful, and very tough, when negotiating the security.

If you sell the *stock* of the business, make sure that, at the very least, you retain a security interest in the stock you sell. This will prevent your buyer from reselling the business without your permission. If the buyer wants to resell, you should have the right to qualify the buyer's buyer, to assure yourself that any new owner will be able to pay the note. Taking a security interest in the stock means that, although you've sold the stock, *you* leave the closing table with the stock certificates, not the buyer. The buyer should receive the certificates and full ownership rights to them only after the note has been fully paid. Your attorney should also file a financing statement with the secretary of state or county clerk, which gives notice to any prospective buyer that the stock can't be sold until your note has been paid.

Here's a trick: Even though you have a security interest in the stock, preventing resale until you are paid, the buyer still will control the corporation. Let's assume that 100 shares represents 100 percent of all the stock of the corporation and you take a security interest in those shares, leaving the closing table with them. What prevents the buyer from turning around and issuing 10 million new shares to himself the day after the closing, in which event your 100 shares represent an insignificant fraction of all the outstanding shares? Nothing, unless your attorney writes an *antidilution* provision into the purchase agreement, preventing the buyer from doing so.

Obtaining a security interest in the corporate stock isn't nearly enough. It doesn't prevent the buyer from reselling the business's *assets* piecemeal or in bulk, reducing the corporation to a shell and rendering the stock worthless. At the very least you should retain a security interest in the business's assets, recording the financing statement with the secretary of state or county clerk. Your security interest should tie up not only the assets you sell but any replacement assets *(after-acquired property)* as well. If the buyer sells a machine (only with your consent, since you'll have a security interest in it), you should have a security interest in the replacement machine. Securing all the assets includes a security interest in the business's *accounts receivable*. If the buyer fails to pay on the note, you should be able to step in and collect these receivables.

Obtaining a security interest in the corporate stock and the business's assets is fairly standard; the buyer should not have a serious objection. What's far more difficult is obtaining a security interest in the buyer's *personal assets,* principally the buyer's home. Depending on the type of business you're selling, the buyer's personal assets may be your principal, or sole, security.

Let's assume you sell your business for $500,000, payable $100,000 in cash at closing and $400,000 by means of a note. If the business has assets that can be sold for $400,000, you shouldn't need to worry. But that's not likely to be the case. We saw in Chapter 5 that the purchase price will likely include a goodwill factor over and above the value of the assets. If your selling a service business, it's probable there're very few assets you'll be able to reduce to cash if you have to. In such a case, the choice is getting a security interest in personal assets or hoping that the note is paid, and taking a tax write-off if it isn't.

A REMINDER: THE BINDING NONDISCLOSURE AGREEMENT

Let's review one important provision in the letter of intent. Although the létter of intent is legally nonbinding, one provision important to the seller should be legally enforceable: the prospective buyer's agreement not to disclose anything the buyer learns about the business, in the event the sale falls through. It's your protection as a seller that the prospective buyer won't steal your trade secrets and go into competition with you. If the prospective buyer balks at signing such a provision, that should be the end of your dealings with that prospective buyer.

Appendix 1

SAMPLE LETTER OF INTENT

Letter of Intent

Peter Purchaser
1050 Glenarm Place
Denver, Colorado 80202

December 31, 1986

Mr. Everett Houston
c/o Houston Sash & Door, Inc.
100 Main St.
Englewood, Colorado 80126

RE: Purchase of Houston Sash & Door, Inc./Letter of Intent

Dear Sir:

This letter, when executed by you in the space provided below, will form our nonbinding Letter of Intent relative to my purchase of the assets, liabilities, business opportunities, and corporate name of Houston Sash & Door, Inc. prior to March 31, 1987. Upon your execution of this letter, we will use our mutual best

191

efforts to execute a binding Purchase Agreement and consummate the sale prior to March 31, 1987, on the following terms:

1.   *Purchase Price.* The total purchase price shall be $1,200,000, payable $200,000 in cash at closing, and $1,000,000 by means of my promissory note in the principal sum of $1,000,000, plus interest at the rate of 12% per annum, payable in 60 equal monthly payments of $22,244.50 per month, principal and interest. The note will be secured by the assets being purchased, including the present and after-acquired accounts receivable. In the event that I elect to effect the purchase through a corporation, I will personally guarantee the note.

2.   *Contingencies.* The consummation of the sale is expressly contingent upon (i) the completion, to my satisfaction, of my full due diligence investigation, (ii) the assignment of the present premises lease, and (iii) the review and approval of respective counsel. The Purchase Agreement will contain the usual representations and warranties relative to financial statements, corporate status, lack of litigation, etc.

3.   *Purchaser's Investigation.* Subsequent to your execution of this letter, my attorney, accountant, and any financial expert I choose may review the books, business operations, and records of the business. We may not contact your premises lessor, suppliers, customers, or employees without your approval, which shall not be unreasonably withheld. In the event that the sale is not consummated prior to March 31, 1987, any information derived by myself, or any individual acting in my behalf, relative to the business shall be retained in strictest confidence and shall not be disclosed, nor may such information be used to your detriment by means of competition or otherwise. This agreement shall be binding upon you and enforceable by you, whether or not a Purchase Agreement is entered into.

4.   *Nondisclosure by Seller.* Until the sale is consummated, or until March 31, 1987, you hereby agree not to divulge to anyone, without any approval, either the fact of this Letter of Intent or the pending of a sale of the business.

If the offer and conditions listed in this letter meet with your approval, please sign in the space provided below and return one copy to me at the above address.

Very truly yours,

Peter Purchaser

Accepted:

_____

Everett Houston

Appendix 2

ANNOTATED PURCHASE AGREEMENT (with Exhibits)

PURCHASE AGREEMENT

1.   THIS AGREEMENT, made and entered into this 31st day of December, 1985, by and among HOUSTON SASH & DOOR, INC., a Colorado corporation ("Seller"), EVERETT HOUSTON ("Houston") and PETER PURCHASER ("Purchaser");

WHEREAS, Seller is in the business of manufacturing, selling and dealing in wooden doors, windows, trusses, frames and other items, and

WHEREAS, Houston is the sole owner of Seller, and

WHEREAS, Seller desires to sell, and Purchaser desires to purchase all of assets, liabilities, business opportunities and name of Seller, and Purchaser desires to purchase the same, on the terms and conditions described herein,

1.   **Purchase and Sale of Business and Assets.** Subject to the terms and conditions set forth in this Agreement, Seller will sell to Purchaser, and Purchaser will purchase, at the Closing, all of the business, assets, liabilities, goodwill and rights of Seller ("Seller's Assets"), including, (i) the assets referred

2.   to in the form of Bill of Sale, attached hereto as Exhibit "1" and (ii) the inventory reflected on the Balance Sheet referred to in Section 5(g) hereof, with any such dispositions of such inventory reflected on the Balance Sheet as shall have occured in the ordinary course of Seller's business between the date thereof

3.   and the Closing. Seller's Assets and inventory shall be conveyed free and clear of all liens and encumbrances excepting only those liabilities and obligations which are expressly to be assumed by Purchaser hereunder and those liens and encumbrances securing the same which are specifically disclosed herein or expressly permitted by the terms hereof.

1.1 Subsequent to Closing, Purchaser shall be entitled to use the name "Houston Sash & Door, Inc." in its trade or business. Seller shall prepare and file whatever assignments are required to assign the name to Purchaser. Subsequent to Closing, Seller shall not use the name Houston Sash & Door, Inc. or any name similar thereto in any trade or business without the permission of Purchaser.

2.   **Purchase Price.** In consideration of the sale of the items described in Section 1, Purchaser will, in full payment thereof, pay to Seller a total price of $1,200,000, payable as follows:

   (i) $200,000 in cash at the Closing, by means of Purchaser's certified check or other certified funds;

   (ii) $1,000,000 by means of the execution and delivery at the Closing of Purchaser's Promissory Note in the
4.   principal amount of $1,000,000, in the form of Exhibit "2," attached hereto.

5.   2.1 The Promissory Note shall be secured by the Seller's Assets, inventory and accounts receivable. At the Closing, Purchaser shall execute a Security Agreement and UCC-1 Financing Statement in form identical to that contained in Exhibits "3" and "4," respectively.

-1-

6.

3. Assumption of Liabilities. Purchaser hereby agrees to assume and pay all of those liabilities of Seller described in Exhibit 5, and to assume those contracts described in Exhibit 6. It is expressly understood that any liabilities or contractual obligations not described in Exhibit 5 and 6 shall remain the sole responsibility of Seller.

7.

3.1 At the Closing, Seller will deliver to buyer's attorney the sum of $10,000, with directions to retain these funds in accordance with the terms of a letter which will be in substantially the form of Exhibit 7, attached hereto, in order to provide for the payment of any liability of Seller not described in Exhibits 5 and 6.

4. Allocation of Assets. The parties hereto agree that the purchase price of the assets shall be as follows. Purchaser and Seller hereby agree to respect the allocations contained herein for all purposes, including federal and state income tax purposes:

8.

Accounts Receivable	$_____
Inventory	$_____
Deports and prepaid items	$_____
Land	$
Buildings	$
Machinery	$
Furniture and Fixtures	$
Automobiles and Light Trucks	$
Corporate Name	$_____
Goodwill	$_____
Agreement Not to Compete	$_____
Other	$_____

9.

5. Closing. The Closing shall occur on March 31, 1986 at 9:30 A.M. at the offices of Seller's counsel. In the event that a party is entitled not to close on the scheduled date because a condition to the Closing set forth herein has not been met, then such party may postpone the Closing from time to time, by giving at least five (5) days' prior notice to the other party, until the condition has been met, but in no event later than April 30, 1986.

6. Seller's Obligations at Closing. At the Closing, Seller and Houston will deliver to Purchaser:

(i) a Bill of Sale duly executed by Seller in the form of Exhibit "1" annexed hereto;

(ii) such other good and sufficient instruments of conveyance, assignment and transfer, in form and substance satisfactory to Purchaser's counsel, as shall be effective to vest in Purchaser good and marketable title to Seller's Assets; and

10.

(iii) all contracts, files and other data and documents pertaining to Seller's Assets, except Seller's minute books and stock ledger records.

-2-

11.

      7. **Representations and Warranties** by **Seller and Houston.** Seller and Houston represent and warrant to Purchaser as follows:

12.

      (a) Organization, Standing and Qualification: Seller is a corporation duly organized, validly existing and in good standing under the laws of Colorado; it has all requisite corporate power and authority and is entitled to carry on its business as now being conducted and to own, lease or operate its properties as and in the places where such business is now conducted and such properties are now owned, leased or operated.

13.

      (b) Subsidiaries. Seller has no subsidiaries. Seller has no interest, and has no commitment to purchase any interest, in any other corporation or in any partnership, joint venture or other business enterprise or entity. The business carried on by Seller has not been conducted through any other direct or indirect subsidiary or affiliate of Houston.

      (c) Transactions with Certain Persons. During the past five years Seller has not, directly or indirectly, purchased, leased from others or otherwise acquired any property or obtained any services from, or sold, leased to others or otherwise disposed of any property or furnished any services to, or otherwise dealt with (i) any shareholder of Seller or (ii) any person, firm or corporation which, directly or indirectly, alone or together with others, controls, is controlled by or is under common control with

14.

Seller or any shareholder of Seller. Seller does not owe any amount to, or have any contract with or commitment to, any of its shareholders, directors, officers, employees or consultants (other than compensation for

15.

current services not yet due and payable and reimbursement of expenses arising in the ordinary course of business), and none of such persons owes any amount to Seller. No part of the property or assets of Houston or any

16.

direct or indirect subsidiary or affiliate of Houston is used by Seller.

17.

      (d) Execution, Delivery and Performance of Agreement; Authority. Neither the execution, delivery nor performance of this Agreement by Seller or Houston will, with or without the giving of notice or the passage of time, or both, conflict with, result in a default, right to accelerate or loss of rights under, or result in creation of any lien, charge or encumbrance pursuant to, any provision of Seller's certificate of incorporation or by-laws or any franchise, mortgage, deed of trust, lease, license, agreement, understanding, law, rule or regulation or any order, judgment or decree to which Seller or Houston is a party or by which any of them may be bound or affected. Seller and Houston have the full power and authority to enter into this Agreement and to carry out the transactions contemplated hereby, all proceedings required to be taken by them or their stockholders to authorize the execution, delivery and performance of this Agreement and the agreements relating hereto have been properly taken and this Agreement constitutes a valid and binding obligation of Seller and Houston.

18.

      (e) Financial Statements. Seller has delivered to Purchaser copies of the following financial statements (hereinafter collectively called the "Financial Statements"), all of which of which are complete and correct, have been prepared from the books and records of Seller in accordance with generally accepted accounting principles consistently applied and maintained throughout the periods indicated and fairly present the financial condition of Seller as at their respective dates and the results of its operations for the periods covered thereby:

(i) unaudited balance sheet of Seller as of December 31, 1984 and of the two fiscal years then ended.

(ii) unaudited balance sheet of Seller as of November 30, 1985, and Seller's unaudited statement of earnings and source and application of funds for the month ending _____, 1985.

Such statements of earnings do not contain any items of special or nonrecurring income or any other income not earned in the ordinary course of business except as expressly specified therein, and such interim financial statements include all adjustments, which consist only of normal recurring accruals, necessary for such fair presentation.

19.   (f) Taxes. All taxes, including, income, property, sales, use, franchise, added value, employees' income withholding and social security taxes, imposed by the United States or by any state, or by any other taxing authority, which are due and payable by Seller, and all interest and penalties thereon, whether disputed or not, have been paid in full, except as disclosed in Exhibit "5," all tax returns required to be filed in connection therewith have been accurately prepared and duly and timely filed and all deposits required by law to be made by Seller with respect to employees' withholding taxes have been duly made. Seller has not been delinquent in the payment of tax, and has no tax deficiency or claim outstanding, proposed or assessed against it, and there is no basis for any such deficiency or claim. Seller's federal income tax returns have been audited and accepted by the Internal Revenue Service for all of its fiscal years through the year ended 1984, there is not now in force any extension of time with respect to the date on which any tax return was or is due to be filed by or with respect to Seller, or any waiver or agreement by it for the extension of time for the assessment of any tax.

20.   (g) Litigation. There is no claim, legal action, governmental investigation or other proceeding, nor any order, decree or judgment in progress, pending or in effect, or to the knowledge of Seller or Houston threatened, against or relating to Seller, its officers, directors or employees, its properties, assets or business or the transactions contemplated by this Agreement, and neither Seller nor Houston knows or has reason to be aware of any basis for the same.

21.   (h) Compliance with Laws and Other Instruments. Seller has complied with all existing laws, rules, regulations, ordinances, orders, judgments and decrees now or hereafter applicable to its business, properties or operations as presently conducted. There are no proposed laws, rules, regulations, ordinances, orders, judgments, decrees, governmental takings, condemnations or other proceedings which would be applicable to its business, operations or properties and which might adversely affect its properties, assets, liabilities, operations or prospects, either before or after the Closing.

22.   (i) Schedules. Attached hereto as Schedule "A" is a separate schedule containing an accurate and complete list and description of:

-4-

(i) All fire, theft, casualty, liability and other insurance policies insuring Seller, specifying with respect to each such policy the name of the insurer, the risk insured against, the limits of coverage, the deductible amount (if any), the premium rate and the date through which coverage will continue by virtue of premiums already paid.

(ii) All sales agency or route distributorship agreements or franchises or agreements providing for the services of an independent contractor to which Seller is a party or by which it is bound.

(iii) All contracts, agreements, commitments or licenses relating to patents, trademarks, trade names, copyrights, inventions, processes, knowhow, formulae or trade secrets to which Seller is a party or by which it is bound.

(iv) All loan agreements, indentures, mortgages, pledges, conditional sale or title retention agreements, security agreements, equipment obligations, guaranties, leases or lease purchase agreements to which Seller is a party or by which it is bound.

(v) All contracts, agreements, commitments or other understandings or arrangements to which Seller is a party or by which it or any of its property is bound or affected but excluding (A) purchase and sales orders and commitments made in the ordinary course of business, and (B) contracts entered into in the ordinary course of business.

(vi) All collective bargaining agreements, employment and consulting agreements, executive compensation plans, bonus, plans, deferred compensation agreements, employee pension plans or retirement plans, employee stock options or stock purchase plans and group life, health and accident insurance and other employee benefit plans, agreements, arrangements or commitments, whether or not legally binding, including, without limitation, holiday, vacation, Christmas and other bonus practices, to which Seller is a party or is bound or which relate to the operation of Seller's business.

23.

(j) Absence of Certain Business Practices. Neither Seller nor any officer, employee or agent of Seller, nor any other person acting on its behalf, has, directly or indirectly, within the past five years given or agreed to give any gift or similar benefit to any customer, supplier, governmental employee or other person who is or may be in a position to help or hinder the business of Seller (or assist Seller in connection with any actual or proposed transaction).

24.

8. Conduct of Business Prior to Closing. (a) Prior to the Closing, Seller shall conduct its business and affairs only in the ordinary course and consistent

with its prior practice and shall maintain, its assets in good condition and
repair and maintain insurance thereon in accordance with present
practices, and Seller and Houston will use their best efforts (i) to preserve
the business and organization of Seller intact, (ii) to keep available to
Purchaser the services of Seller's present officers, employees, agents and
independent contractors, (iii) to preserve for the benefit of Purchaser the
goodwill of Seller's suppliers, customers, landlords and others having
business relations with it, (iv) to cooperate with Purchaser and use
reasonable efforts to assist Purchaser in obtaining the consent of any
landlord or other party to any lease or contract with Seller where the
consent of such landlord or other party may be required by reason of the
transactions contemplated hereby. Without limiting the generality of the
foregoing, prior to the Closing Seller will not without Purchaser's prior
written approval:

> (i) change its certificate of incorporation or by-laws or
> merge or consolidate or obligate itself to do so with or into any
> other entity;

> (ii) take any actions of the type described in Section 7 or
> which would be inconsistent with the representations and
> warranties contained therein.

25.   9. **Access to Information and Documents.** Upon reasonable notice and
during regular business hours, Seller will give Purchaser and Purchaser's
attorneys, accountants and other representatives full access to Seller's personnel
and all properties, documents, contracts, books and records of Seller and will
furnish Purchaser with copies of such documents (certified by Seller's officers if
so requested) and with such information with respect to the affairs of Seller as
Purchaser may from time to time request, and Purchaser will not improperly
disclose the same prior to the Closing.

26.   10. **Conditions Precedent to Purchaser's Obligations.** All obligations of
Purchaser hereunder are subject, at the option of Purchaser, to the fulfillment of
each of the following conditions at or prior to the Closing, and Seller and
Houston shall exert their best efforts to cause such condition to be so fulfilled:

> (a) All representations and warranties of Seller and Houston
> contained herein or in any document delivered pursuant hereto shall be true
> and correct in all material respects when made and shall be deemed to
> have been made again at and as of the date of the Closing, and shall then
> be true and correct in all material respects except for changes in the
> ordinary course of business after the date hereof in conformity with the
> covenants and agreements contained herein.

> (b) All covenants, agreements and obligations required by the terms
> of this Agreement to be performed by Seller or Houston at or before the
> Closing shall have been duly and properly performed in all material
> respects.

> (c) Since the date of this Agreement there shall not have occurred
> any material adverse change in the condition (financial or otherwise),
> business, properties, assets or prospects of Seller.

-6-

(d) Seller shall have obtained written consent to the transfer or assignment to Purchaser of all consignment agreements, licenses, leases and other material contracts of Seller (other than immaterial purchaser and sales orders in the ordinary course of business) where the consent of any other party to any such contract may, in the option of Purchaser's counsel, be required for such assignment or transfer.

27.   11. **Bulk Sales.** Purchaser shall give notice, in compliance with the Uniform Commercial Code, of the bulk transfer contemplated by this Agreement. Seller shall furnish Purchaser with the information necessary to prepare this notice, including all names and business addresses used by it within the last 3 years, at least 20 days prior to the Closing.

28.   12. **Indemnification.** Seller and Houston, jointly and severally, hereby indemnify, against and in respect of (and shall on demand reimburse Purchaser for):

(i) any and all loss, liability or damage suffered or incurred by Purchaser by reason of any untrue representation, breach of warranty or nonfulfillment of any covenant by Seller or Houston contained herein;

(ii) any and all loss, liability or damage suffered or incurred by Purchaser in respect of or in connection with any liabilities of Seller not specifically assumed by Purchaser pursuant to the terms of this Agreement;

(iii) any and all debts, liabilities or obligations of Seller, direct or indirect, fixed, contingent or otherwise, which exist at or as of the Balance Sheet Date or which arise after the Balance Sheet Date which are based upon or arise from any act, transaction, circumstance, sale of goods or services, state of facts, or other condition which occurred or existed on or before the Balance Sheet Date, whether or not then known, due or payable, except to the extent reflected or reserved against on the face of the Balance Sheet (excluding the notes thereto);

(iv) any and all debts, liabilities or obligations of Seller, direct or indirect, fixed, contingent or otherwise, which exist at or as of the date of the Closing hereunder or which arise after the Closing but which are based upon or arise from any act, transaction, circumstance, sale of goods or services, state of facts or other condition which occurred or existed on or before the date of the Closing, whether or not then known, due or payable, except to the extent reflected or reserved against on the face of the Balance Sheet (excluding the notes thereto) or incurred after the Balance Sheet Date in conformity with the representations, warranties and covenants contained in this Agreement (or a Schedule hereto);

(v) any and all actions, suits, proceedings, claims, demands, assessments, judgments, costs and expenses,

-7-

including, without limitation, legal fees and expenses, incident
to any of the foregoing or incurred in investigating or
attempting to avoid the same or to oppose the imposition
thereof, or in enforcing this indemnity.

IN WITNESS WHEREOF, the parties hereto have caused this Agreement to
be duly executed as of the day and year first above written.

HOUSTON SASH & DOOR, INC.

29.   By: _____   _____
        Its President   PETER PURCHASER

Attest:_____
      Secretary

EVERETT HOUSTON _____

Recorded at _____ o'clock _____ M., _____
Reception No. _____ _____   Recorder.

BILL OF SALE

KNOW ALL MEN BY THESE PRESENTS, That

Houston Sash & Door, Inc.   of the
    *County of   Arapahoe   , State of Colorado,
(Seller), for and in consideration of
    Ten and No/100——————————————————— Dollars,
to him in hand paid, at or before the ensealing or delivery of these presents by

Peter Purchaser   of the   City and *
County of   Denver   , in the State of Colorado,
(Buyer), the receipt of which is hereby acknowledged, has bargained and sold, and by these presents does grant and convey unto
the said Buyer, his personal representatives, successors and assigns, the following property, goods and chattels, to wit:

1 Columbine Model 800-A Milling Machine
3 Desk-top Model 900 Milling Machines
5 Lathes
2 Bench presses with tools and chucks
2 Model 100 Die-Presses
10,500+ running feet of lumber of various grades
250 completed trusses
1 Bonding Machine
2 Metal desks and chairs
3 Filing cabinets (Metal)
3 Filing Cabinets (Plastic)
2 Typewriters
1 Water cooler
Assorted tooks, dyes, soldering equipment
5 Barrels of nails (assorted)
1 Model 22 forklift
1 1974 Chevy Van

located at   100 Main St., Englewood, Colorado 80001

TO HAVE AND TO HOLD the same unto the said Buyer, his personal representatives, successors and assigns, forever. The
said Seller covenants and agrees to and with the Buyer, his personal representatives, successors and assigns, to WARRANT AND
DEFEND the sale of said property, goods and chattels, against all and every person or persons whomever. When used herein, the
singular shall include the plural, the plural the singular, and the use of any gender shall be applicable to all genders.
IN WITNESS WHEREOF, the Seller has executed this Bill of Sale this _____ day of _____ , 19 _____ .
                              HOUSTON SASH & DOOR, INC.

                              By : _____
                              _____

        STATE OF COLORADO,   }
        _____ County of _____ } ss.

The foregoing instrument was acknowledged before me this   day of   , 19
My commission expires
Witness my hand and Official seal.

                              _____
                              Notary Public

*If in Denver, insert "City and."

No. 35A. Rev. 9-83. BILL OF SALE

Exhibit 1

PROMISSORY NOTE

$1,000,000   March 31, 1987

FOR VALUE RECEIVED, Peter Purchaser ("Maker") promises to pay to Houston Sash & Door, Inc. ("Payee") or order, the principal sum of One Million Dollars ($1,000,000) with interest on the unpaid principal balance from the date of this Note, until paid, at the rate of twelve per cent (12%) per annum. Said principal and interest shall be payable at 8500 E. Orchard Ave., Englewood, Colorado 80001, or at such other place as the Payee, or legal holder or owner (hereinafter "Payee") of the Note may from time to time designate in writing. Principal and interest shall be payable in 60 consecutive monthly payments of $22,244.50, principal and interest, due on the first day of each month commencing on May 1, 1987, with the balance of principal and accrued interest due and payable on May 1, 1992.

1. *Prepayment.* This note may be prepaid, at any time, in whole or in part, without penalty, provided that the Note is not in default, and provided further that any prepayment shall first be allocated toward a reduction of principal.

2. *Late Fee.* Monthly payments of interest and/or principal which are not received by Payee by the fifth day of any month for the preceding month shall include a late fee of 4% of any amount not paid by said fifth day, and shall be added to the late amount.

3. *Default.* If this Note is not paid when due or declared due hereunder, the principal and accrued interest thereon shall draw interest at the rate of eighteen percent (18%) per annum, and failure to make any payment of principal or interest under this Note when due shall cause the whole of the unpaid principal amount of this Note and accrued interest to become due and payable at once, or the interest to be counted as principal, at the option of the Payee.

4. *Waiver of Presentment and Dishonor; Fees for Collection.* Maker and all parties who at any time may be liable or become liable hereon in any capacity, jointly and severally, waive presentment

for payment, any extension of time of payment and partial payments before, at or after maturity, and if this Note or interest thereon is not paid when due, or suit is brought, agree to pay all reasonable costs of collection, including a reasonable amount of money for attorney's fees.

5. *Joint and Several Obligation.* The rights and remedies of the Payee as provided herein shall be cumulative and concurrent and may be pursued singly, successively, or together. The failure to exercise any such right, remedy, or election shall in no event be construed as a waiver or release of such rights, remedies, or election or of the rights to exercise them at any later time. This note is to be construed according to the laws of the State of Colorado.

This note shall be the joint and several obligation of all makers, sureties, guarantors, and endorsers, and shall be binding upon them and their respective heirs, personal representatives, successors, and assigns. Whenever used herein, the words "Maker," or "Payee," shall be deemed to include their respective heirs, personal representatives, successors, and assigns.

6. *Security.* The indebtedness evidenced by this note is secured by a Security Agreement of even date in certain assets, including after-acquired assets.

7. *Notices.* All notices or other communications required or permitted under this Note shall be in writing and shall be given by delivery, or by registered or certified mail, return receipt requested, postage prepaid, directed as follows:

If intended for Payee, to:
Everett Houston
8500 E. Orchard Avenue
Englewood, Colorado 80001

If intended to Maker, to:
Peter Purchaser
1060 Glenarm Place
Denver, Colorado 80202

Any such notice shall be deemed to be given when personally delivered or, in the case of service by mail, on the day of actual delivery as shown on the addressee's registered or certified mail receipt or forty-eight (48) hours after the date of mailing, whichever is the earlier. Any party may give notice at any time to change the address to which future notices are to be sent by giving notice as hereinabove provided.

_____

Peter Purchaser, Maker

Due: May 1, 1992

Exhibit 2

STATE OF COLORADO

UNIFORM COMMERCIAL CODE — SECURITY AGREEMENT

Debtor:

Name: Peter Purchaser

Address: Residence: 1050 Glenarm Place   Denver   Colorado   80202
No.   Street   City   State

Business: Same
No.   Street   City   State

Secured Party:

Name: Houston Sash & Door, Inc.

Address: 100 Main St.   Englewood,   Colorado   80126
No.   Street   City   State

Debtor, for consideration, hereby grants to Secured Party a security interest in the following property and any and all additions, accessions and substitutions thereto or therefor (hereinafter called the "COLLATERAL"): All inventory, furniture and fixtures, leasehold improvements, equipment and accounts receivable now in the possession of Houston Sash & Door, Inc. or hereafter acquired, wherever situate.

To secure payment of the indebtedness evidenced by ____a____ certain promissory note ____ of even date herewith, payable to the Secured Party, or order, as follows: A promissory note of even date in the principal sum of $1,000.00 bearing interest at the rate of 12% per annum, payable in 60 monthly installments of $22,244.50.

DEBTOR EXPRESSLY WARRANTS AND COVENANTS:

1. That except for the security interest granted hereby Debtor is, or to the extent that this agreement states that the Collateral is to be acquired after the date hereof, will be, the owner of the Collateral free from any adverse lien, security interest or encumbrances; and that Debtor will defend the Collateral against all claims and demands of all persons at anytime claiming the same or any interest therein.

2. The Collateral is used or bought primarily for:
☐ Personal, family or household purposes;
☐ Use in farming operations;
☒ Use in business.

3. That Debtor's residence is as stated above, and the Collateral will be kept at

100 Main St.   Englewood   Arapahoe   Colorado
No. and Street   City   County   State

4. If any of the Collateral is crops, oil, gas, or minerals to be extracted or timber to be cut, or goods which are or are to become fixtures, said Collateral concerns the following described real estate situate in the __N/A__ County of __N/A__ and State of Colorado, to wit:

No. UCC 1205. Rev. 3-87.   SECURITY AGREEMENT   Bradford Publishing, 5825 W 6th Ave., Lakewood, CO 80214 — (303) 233-6900   3-87

Exhibit 3

5.   Promptly to notify Secured Party of any change in the location of the Collateral.

6.   To pay all taxes and assessments of every nature which may be levied or assessed against the Collateral.

7.   Not to permit or allow any adverse lien, security interest or encumbrance whatsoever upon the Collateral and not to permit the same to be attached or replevined.

8.   That the Collateral is in good condition, and that he will, at his own expense, keep the same in good condition and from time to time, forthwith, replace and repair all such parts of the Collateral as may be broken, worn out, or damaged without allowing any lien to be created upon the Collateral on account of such replacement or repairs, and that the Secured Party may examine and inspect the Collateral at any time, wherever located.

9.   That he will not use the Collateral in violation of any applicable statutes, regulations or ordinances.

10.   The Debtor will keep the Collateral at all times insured against risks of loss or damage by fire (including so-called extended coverage), theft and such other casualties as the Secured Party may reasonably require, including collision in the case of any motor vehicle, all in such amounts, under such forms of policies, upon such terms, for such periods, and written by such companies or underwriters as the Secured Party may approve, losses in all cases to be payable to the Secured Party and the Debtor as their interest may appear. All policies of insurance shall provide for at least ten days' prior written notice of cancellation to the Secured Party; and the Debtor shall furnish the Secured Party with certificates of such insurance or other evidence satisfactory to the Secured Party as to compliance with the provisions of this paragraph. The Secured Party may act as attorney for the Debtor in making, adjusting and settling claims under or cancelling such insurance and endorsing the Debtor's name on any drafts drawn by insurers of the Collateral.

UNTIL DEFAULT Debtor may have possession of the Collateral and use it in any lawful manner, and upon default Secured Party shall have the immediate right to the possession of the Collateral.

DEBTOR SHALL BE IN DEFAULT under this agreement upon the happening of any of the following events or conditions:

(a) default in the payment or performance of any obligation, covenant or liability contained or referred to herein or in any note evidencing the same;

(b) the making or furnishing of any warranty, representation or statement to Secured Party by or on behalf of Debtor which proves to have been false in any material respect when made or furnished;

(c) loss, theft, damage, destruction, sale or encumbrance to or of any of the Collateral, or the making of any levy seizure or attachment thereof or thereon;

(d) death, dissolution, termination or existence, insolvency, business failure, appointment of a receiver of any part of the property of, assignment for the benefit of creditors by, or the commencement of any proceeding under any bankruptcy or insolvency laws of, by or against Debtor or any guarantor or surety for Debtor.

UPON SUCH DEFAULT and at any time thereafter, or if it deems itself insecure, Secured Party may declare all Obligations secured hereby immediately due and payable and shall have the remedies of a secured party under Article 9 of the Colorado Uniform Commercial Code. Secured Party may require Debtor to assemble the Collateral and deliver or make it available to Secured Party at a place to be designated by Secured Party which is reasonably convenient to both parties. Expenses of retaking, holding, preparing for sale, selling or the like shall include Secured Party's reasonable attorney's fees and legal expenses.

No waiver by Secured Party of any default shall operate as a waiver of any other default or of the same default on a future occasion. The taking of this security agreement shall not waive or impair any other security said Secured Party may have or hereafter acquire for the payment of the above indebtedness, nor shall the taking of any such additional security waive or impair this security agreement; but said Secured Party may resort to any security it may have in the order it may deem proper, and notwithstanding any collateral security, Secured Party shall retain its rights of set-off against Debtor.

All rights of Secured Party hereunder shall inure to the benefit of its successors and assigns; and all promises and duties of Debtor shall bind his heirs, executors or administrators or his or its successors or assigns. If there be more than one Debtor, their liabilities hereunder shall be joint and several.

Date this _____31st_____ day of _____March_____, 19 _87_____ .

Debtor: Secured Party:*

_____   _____

PETER PURCHASER

_____   _____

*If this Security Agreement is intended to serve as a financing statement secured party as well as the debtor must sign.

STATE OF COLORADO
UNIFORM COMMERCIAL CODE — FINANCING STATEMENT - COLORADO U.C.C.-1 (Rev. 1-78)

INSTRUCTIONS
1. PLEASE TYPE this form. Do not write in Box 3.
2. If collateral is CROPS, state in Box 4, "The above described crops are growing or are to be grown on: (Describe Real Estate concerned).
3. If collateral is or will become FIXTURES, or is TIMBER TO BE CUT, or is MINERALS OR OTHER SUBSTANCES OF VALUE WHICH MAY BE EXTRACTED FROM THE EARTH OR ACCOUNTS RESULTING FROM THE SALE THEREOF AT THE WELLHEAD OR MINEHEAD, CHECK ☒ "This Financing Statement is to be filed for record in the Real Estate records." in Box 4 and state if applicable. "The above goods are, or are to become, fixtures on (describe real estate)," or where appropriate, substitute either, "The above timber is standing on (describe real estate)," or, "The above minerals or other substances of value which may be extracted from the earth or accounts resulting from the sale thereof at the wellhead or minehead of the well or mine located on (describe real estate)." Describe real estate concerned sufficient as if it were contained in a mortgage of the real estate to give constructive notice of the mortgage under the law of this State. If the debtor does not have an interest of record in the realty, give the name of a record owner of the real estate concerned in Box 4.
4. If the space provided for any item on the form is inadequate, the item should be continued on additional sheets, that are 8½x11.
   Please do not staple or tape additional sheets directly on this form.
5. Remove Secured Party and Debtor copies, and send 3 copies with interleaved carbon paper still intact to the filing officer.
6. At the time of original filing, the filing officer will return third copy as an acknowledgment. If acknowledgment copy is to be returned to other than the Secured Party, please enclose a self-addressed envelope.

IMPORTANT — Read instructions before filling out form

This FINANCING STATEMENT is presented for filing pursuant to the Uniform Commercial Code.	3. For Filing Officer (Date, Time, Number and Filing Office)

1. Debtor(s) Name and Mailing Address:	2. Secured Party(ies) Name and Address:	
Peter Purchaser 1050 Glenarm Place Denver, CO 80202	Houston Sash & Door, Inc. 100 Main Street Englewood, CO 80126	

4. This Financing Statement covers the following types (or items) of property:
(WARNING: If collateral is crops, fixtures, timber, or minerals or other substances to be extracted or accounts resulting from the sale thereof, read instructions above.)   All inventory, furniture, and fixtures, leasehold improvements, equipment and accounts receivables, presently owned or hereafter acquired by Debtor.

5. Name and address of Assignee of Secured Party:

Check only if applicable
☐ This Statement is to be filed for record in the real estate records.
☒ Products of collateral are also covered. ☐ Proceeds of collateral are also covered.

6. This statement is signed by the Secured Party instead of the Debtor to perfect a security interest in collateral
(Please check appropriate box)
☐ already subject to a security interest in another jurisdiction when it was brought into this state, or when the debtor's location was changed to this state;
☐ which is proceeds of the original collateral described above in which a security interest was perfected;
☐ as to which the filing has lapsed; or
☐ acquired after a change of name, identity or corporate structure of the debtor.

7. Check only if applicable: ☐ The Debtor is a transmitting utility.

Use whichever signature line is applicable.

HOUSTON SASH & DOOR, INC.

PETER PURCHASER

By:

Signature(s) of Debtor(s)   Signature(s) of Secured Party(ies)

Form approved by the Secretary of State and the County Clerks and Recorders Association

(1) FILING OFFICER COPY

No. 601. COLORADO FORM U.C.C. 1 (REV. 1-78)
Bradford Publishing (303) 233-6900

Exhibit 4

SCHEDULE OF LIABILITIES

The following represents the trade and other debts of Seller other than the liabilities contained in Seller's premises lease, which Purchaser hereby agrees to assume. This schedule is prepared pursuant to Section 3 of the Purchase Agreement, and is incorporated therein by reference:

Creditor	Amount (as of December 31, 1986)
Acme Lumber Co.	$55,419.31
Baker Building Supply, Inc.	49,011.00
Al Tools, Inc.	8,439.00
Johnson Hardware Co.	900.00
Colorado Maintenance, Inc.	841.42
Rocky Mountain Truckers, Inc.	5,581.00
Mountain Bell	862.40
Ace Office Supply Co.	191.21

Exhibit 5

SCHEDULE OF CONTRACTS

The following represents the contracts to which Seller is a party. Purchaser will assume the obligations of Seller. This schedule is prepared pursuant to Section 3 of the Purchase Agreement, and is incorporated herein by reference:

1.   Contract with U.S. Homebuilders, dated June 1, 1984.

2.   Contract of general liability insurance with Rocky Mountain Insurance, dated July 1, 1984.

3.   Employment Agreement of Ralph Smith, dated January 1, 1985.

Exhibit 6

Peter Purchaser
1050 Glenarm Place
Denver, Colorado 80202

Boris, Klueger, Nemkov & Jahde, P.C.
1325 So. Colorado Boulevard, Suite 308
Denver, Colorado 80222

RE: Houston Sash & Door, Inc.; Purchase Agreement

Gentlemen:

Please find enclosed the sum of $10,000.00, which you are hereby directed to deposit on behalf of myself and the Seller, Houston Sash & Door, Inc., pursuant to the terms of the above-referenced Purchase Agreement.

In the event that you are notified by the Seller or its shareholder, Mr. Everett Houston, that any debt listed in Exhibit 5 or any obligation arising out of any agreement to which Seller is a party pursuant to Exhibit 6 is not paid in accordance with its terms, you are hereby directed to make such payment directly to the appropriate party (and not to Seller), pursuant to written direction of Seller.

To the extent all or any part of the aforesaid $10,000.00 remains in your trust account on December 31, 1987, you are directed to remit the balance to the undersigned.

Very truly yours,

Peter Purchaser

Exhibit 7

Appendix **3**
SAMPLE BUSINESS PLAN

AUTHOR'S NOTE:

What follows is a model business plan prepared principally in order to induce a lender to commit the funds requisite to the purchase of an existing business. A similar business plan would be used to induce a venture capital firm to make an investment in a business.

A business plan is intended to convey two impressions: (1) that the prospective owners have fully familiarized themselves with every aspect of the business, and (2) that they are fully equipped, by education, experience and expertise to run the business successfully. This business plan doesn't tell merely the "good" side of the story. Potential risks and hazards are discussed, but in each instance the new owners' plans for minimizing these risks and hazards are also discussed.

There's no magic formula for writing business plans and no set order for disclosure. A business plan for a different business written for a different purpose (e.g., a plan written to induce an investment in a start-up business) would not necessarily follow the same format. Don't be locked into or attempt to clone any other business plan.

The projections and financial statements that normally would accompany the business plan are on pages 32, 33, 64–65, and 68.

215

HOUSTON SASH & DOOR, INC.

Business Plan
October 1, 1987

CONFIDENTIAL

This Business Plan is prepared only for the person to whom it is presented, and may not be reproduced, broadcast, or disclosed, in whole or in part, for any reason.

Prepared by:
Peter Purchaser
Ralph Brown
Ed Smith

TABLE OF CONTENTS

Section 1: Purpose of Business Plan

We, the undersigned, Peter Purchaser, Ralph Brown and Ed Smith, have entered into negotiations for the purchase of the assets, business and name of Houston Sash & Door, Inc., a Colorado corporation, which is engaged in the manufacture and sale of wooden windows, doors, trusses and other components of residential dwellings, to general contractors.

Toward that end, we have executed a non-binding Letter of Intent (See Exhibit 1) to purchase the business on the following terms:

1. $200,000 in cash.

2. $1,000,000 by means of a Promissory Note secured by the assets of the business.

In representing this business plan, the undersigned desire to borrow the sum of $450,000, the sum required for the cash down-payment, ($200,000) and an additional $250,000 for expansion of equipment, inventory and sales force. We are confident that, even as presently managed, cash flow from the business is sufficient to adequately service this debt.

The following Business Plan contains our expectations and intentions with respect to the operations of Houston Sash & Door, Inc. should we purchase the business. THIS IS INFORMATION WHICH COULD BENEFIT A COMPETITOR AND HENCE MUST BE KEPT CONFIDENTIAL.

Peter Purchaser
Ralph Brown
Ed Smith

Section 2: Summary of Existing Business

General

Houston Sash & Door, Inc., (the "Company") 100 Main St., Englewood, Colorado, has been engaged in the manufactⅎre of wooden building components (principally windows, doors and trusses) since 1966. Its founder and sole shareholder since inception is Mr. Everett Houston, age 66. Mr. Houston desires to retire from business and consequently is seeking to sell the business.

The Company sells its products exclusively to home builders. In 1985, 60% of its sales were to U.S. Homebuilders, Inc., Denver, 30% to American Homes, Inc., Denver, and the balance to 8 other home builders. Less than 1% of sales were to home owners and lumber yards.

Summary Financial Data

The Company experienced a rapid increase in sales during the building boom of the 1970's, jumping from approximately $60,000 in sales in 1970 to $1,341,300 in 1980. Since 1980, sales remained steady rising to $1,881,117 in 1985. However net income declined to $280,397 in 1985 from $332,815 in 1984, the first year in which the Company experienced in decline in net income.

We believe that the leveling off of sales and the most recent decline in earnings is a direct consequence of the owner's understandable reluctance to invest in new plant or machinery or to seek to generate additional accounts, considering the owner's desire to leave the business. However, we also believe that present accounts have been adequately serviced and are not in danger of being lost.

Selected financial information follows, which summarizes the Financial Statements contained in Exhibit 2:

	Fiscal Years Ended December 31	
	1985	1984
Operating Data		
Revenues	$1,881,117	$1,832,286
Net Profit	$ 280,397	$ 332,815
Total Assets	$ 822,658	$ 568,566
Current Liabilities	$ 86,243	$ 157,548
Stockholder's Equity	$ 691,415	$ 411,018

Personnel

The Company employs 5 employees engaged in milling operations, including one foreman, Mr. Ralph Smith. Mr. Smith is compensated pursuant to an employment agreement which expires on January 1, 1988, at a rate of $5,000 per month. The Company employs one outside salesman who is compensated on a salaried basis. In addition, the Company employs one full-time and two part-time office clerical employees.

We believe that operations personnel are under-utilized, and that certain cut-backs could be made. However, we believe that at least two additional sales persons are required, who should be compensated on a commission basis. Consequently, we do not feel that any savings can be realized with respect to compensation expense. Indeed, compensation expense should be increased.

Plant and Equipment

The Company's operations and administrative functions are conducted at 100 Main St., Englewood, Colorado, at a 12,900+ square foot facility leased from AA Realty, Inc. The lease expires on January 1, 1990. The current annual rent is $55,753 per year, which is above the current market by at least 40%. The plant is adequate for current operations and for expansion.

Equipment is adequate for current operations and for expansion, with the exception of the Columbine 800-A Milling Machine, which is obsolescent. The replacement cost of this machine is approximately $40,000.

Competition and Markets

The Company is one of three milling operations in the Denver area, and is considered the leader in the terms of sales. The other local milling operations, Rocky Mountain Door, Inc. and Columbine Sash & Door, Inc. are both engaged in specialty milling operations for custom-designed homes, and hence represent competition for only a minor segment of the Denver home-building market. The Company mills only pine lumber, whereas only a minority of the milling operations of its two competitors are in pine. Consequently, the Company has no local competition with respect to mass produced homes. Local homebuilders prefer to use local suppliers in order to reduce shipping charges and to control quality. Consequently, larger milling operations located outside of Denver have not, and are not likely to represent competition to the Company.

Sales are tied, to an extent, to home-building activity. The slackening in home-building during the last 5 years in the Denver area has resulted in a leveling off of sales. However, as home-building activity has slackened off, the Company's cost of its principal inventory component, pine lumber, has levelled off.

We believe that present management has failed to capitalize on a growing potential market, being direct sales to the retail public. Such sales could, we believe, increase sales by at least 20% annually and increase net income by 15% annually.

Business Risks

We have identified one particular business risk in the manner in which the Company presently conducts its business: 90% of the Company's sales are to two major homebuilders, and 60% to one homebuilder. If one or both of these customers were to either discontinue operations or use other suppliers, it would have a severe impact upon the Company's revenues and profits.

We intend to alleviate this risk by diversifying the Company's operations, by 1) entering into the market throughout the front range of Colorado, lessening the percentage of sales to the Denver market, 2) entering into the "specialty millwork" market, selling to smaller custom builders and 3) selling windows and other building products to retail customers at the Company's Englewood facility. See "Business Goals." (Section 3)

Section 3:   Business Goals

We believe that the Company's revenues can be substantially and quickly increased in three areas, at a minimal incremental cost and at its present facility. These areas are:

1.   Aggressive marketing directed at home builders located in the front-range of Colorado (Fort Collins to Pueblo) but outside of the Denver area, who are presently serviced by smaller milling operations none of whom provide the broad range of products as does the Company, at prices generally higher than does the Company.

2.   Entry into the specialty milling market, in direct competition with Rocky Mountain Door, Inc. and Columbine Sash & Door, Inc.

3.   Sales of windows directly to home owners engaged in either building their own homes or "fixing up" their residences.

In addition, we believe that savings can be effected in a number of areas. We believe that at present, quality, inventory and accounting control is poor and can be improved by implementing a number of internal controls. These goals are discussed below:

1.   Marketing Directed at Homebuilders Outside of Denver.

Since its inception, the Company has sold its products exclusively to the larger homebuilders in the Denver area. The Company sells more of its products to the smaller homebuilders throughout the front-range of Colorado, i.e. in Fort Collins, Boulder, Colorado Springs or Pueblo. These homebuilders are serviced by smaller local milling operations who offer a narrower range of products, at higher prices and with longer turn-around times.

We believe that the incremental costs in attempting to gain a foothold in these markets would be two-fold: 1) the additional sales and promotional expense, and 2) the additional transportation costs, once the additional volume has been obtained.

We propose to handle the incremental costs of sales promotions as conservatively as possible. Since there will be three business owners, as opposed to the present one, one of the three new owners will visit the general contractors in each locale in order to induce sales. Consequently, the Company will not incur incremental salary or commission charges. The only incremental charges will be travel and expense costs, which will be minimal. In addition, a certain amount of increased advertising will be budgeted, targeted in those cities that are not serviced at present.

The second incremental item of expense will be additional freight charges required to ship longer distances. No new accounts outside of Denver will be accepted unless and until the total volume outside of Denver is sufficient to cover increased overhead. In other words, any sales generated outside of Denver must be self-sustaining at inception.

There are no plans at present to generate sales outside of the front range of Denver. However, if substantial sales are generated in the front range, which have the effect of increasing profitability, the Company may attempt to generate sales to the Western slope or into Kansas, Nebraska and/or Wyoming. Again, the Company will not expand into new territories unless these sales are self-sustaining at inception.

2. Entry into the Specialty Milling Market.

Since its inception, the Company has sold its products exclusively to larger local builders of "tract" homes. The Company has followed this strategy largely due to its ease of administration. The Company was required to deal with the needs of only a small number of home builders and their general or subcontractors. As a result, a substantial percentage of business was repeat business of outstanding orders, lowering the per unit cost of each running foot of lumber sold and thereby increasing the per unit profit margin. However, this strategy has placed an artificial ceiling on revenues and has made the Company dependent upon sales of homes at the lower end of the market. This in turn ties sales to fluctuations in the Denver housing market, which recently has been soft. All of this is a result of the present owner's lack of desire to increase sales.

The specialty market is presently serviced by two local millwork firms, Rocky Mountain Door and Columbine Sash & Door, both of which are considerably smaller than the Company.

The specialty market consists of doors, windows, woodworking, bannisters and other items included in "custom" homes. These custom homes are usually constructed by smaller homebuilders, some of whom may build only one or two homes per year. As opposed to the pine lumber with which the Company works exclusively, specialty items are constructed of oak, cherrywood, cedar and a host of other woods, as well as pine. In all cases, specialty items are custom-designed (although often a design repeats from particular builders) and require milling that is done to more exact tolerances and requiring more finely-tuned procedures, occasionally on different equipment.

The specialty market is extremely profitable for those firms engaged in it, since the markup item is greater than the Company's markup.

We believe that the Company has the plant capacity and the expertise to enter into and successfully compete with existing firms. The only incremental costs would be the purchase of a small amount of specialty milling equipment, estimated at $30,000.

There is one _defensive_ strategy which militates in favor of entry into this market. Millwork operators have historically lived in fear that plastic or other materials will begin to compete with millwork. Although this has not yet occurred, the possibility still exists. Although plastic doors and windows might one day become a serious competitor with millwork geared toward the tract builder, there is almost no possibility that plastic or other cheap materials will compete with specialty millwork.

3. Retail Sales to Homeowners.

The Company sells almost no product at retail. The only retail sales are incidental sales of a few running feet of lumber to those individuals who are willing to pick out and transport lumber on their own. The Company conducts no advertising aimed at the retail market, and practically discourages it.

There are a number of extremely small and poorly capitalized firms in the Denver market who sell and install finished windows to homeowners who are either building their own homes (i.e. acting as their own general contractors) or who are remodeling their homes. The sale and installation is priced to the customer as a package. Considering the price of the window to the installer, and the minimal time involved in installation, the markup is extraordinary. Indeed, the principal cost involved is advertising, which is usually conducted by means of door-to-door or telephone solicitation.

We believe that the Company has the ability to substantially under-cut the prices charged by these firms, since the Company, which builds the windows itself and would be selling them directly to the end-user, would be eliminating the middleman's huge markup.

Initially, entry into the market would entail a substantial amount of advertising, estimated at $50,000. Thereafter, advertising would be minimal. WE BELIEVE THE COMPANY CAN BECOME DOMINANT IN THIS SECTOR IN DENVER WITHIN 12 MONTHS.

In addition to the sales of windows, we foresee that sales of windows at retail would spin-off other sources of income. There is easily enough space at the present facility for a loading bay, counter, waiting area and storage area for retail customers. Once a steady flow of retain customers is generated, sales of hardware items such as power saws and other small hand tools, metal brackets, screws, etc. would naturally follow. All of the foregoing could be accomplished by employing no more than one counterman and a stockboy. We believe that the profits from the ancillary items alone would be sufficient to cover the incremental labor costs entailed in dealing directly with the public.

4. Quality, Inventory and Accounting Controls.

At present, the Company's accounting, inventory and quality controls are almost non-existent. This accounting is so poor that it is presently impossible to gauge how much could be saved if certain basic controls were instituted. Although we have no evidence that any theft of inventory occurs, controls are so lacking that if theft were to occur it would be impossible to spot, since there is no accounting or control of the inflow or outgo of product. The following controls would be instituted:

1. The Company would begin accounting on a product-by-product basis. At present, management has no idea what is the relative profitability of any of its products, or if any of its products are unprofitable.

2. Purchaser would be checked to assure that they conform to orders and are of conforming quality. At present, non-conforming lumber finds its way

into furnished windows and doors and is returned ("backcharged") to the Company. At that point, there is no way to demand a credit from the supplier, since there is no accounting or control of purchase orders.

3. Inventory is ordered when it "appears low," leading to delays in production. The Company has no idea which items move more quickly than others, leading to the possibility (though there is presently no way of knowing) that certain items have a long shelf life, resulting in needless cash expenditures.

We have observed all of the foregoing as a result of our inquiries and due diligence investigation. We are confident that a more complete analysis of operation, once we have assumed control, would result in additional accounting controls and further savings.

Section 4: Organization and Personnel

1. Present Organizational Chart.

The present organization of the Company is as follows:

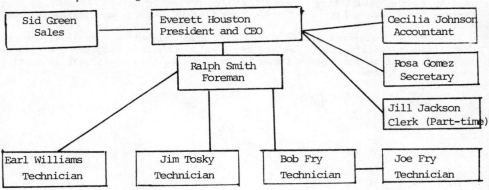

2. Analysis of Personnel.

Present personnel are sufficient to conduct current operations and to handle any increase in production, with the exception that an additional counterman and stockboy would be required in the event that retail sales are made. The present outside salesman, Sid Green, could handle sales calls throughout the front range, since his present duties are by and large limited to consulting with current customers.

Company personnel are not unionized, and there has been no unionization activity. Present work force is stable, with little turnover except for part-timers.

Mr. Ralph Smith, the foreman, is the only key employee. The three technicians, who handle all of the actual milling and construction operations, are semi-skilled, and can be trained in a period of 1-2 weeks, assuming they have successfully completed a high school shop course. Mr. Smith is a vital component to the business, and would be difficult to replace. He is intimately unacquainted with all aspects of the Company's operations, the needs of the Company's customers, and the needs and vagaries of the Company's suppliers. He currently is employed under an Employment Agreement which will expire on January 1, 1988, unless renewed prior thereto.

3. Analysis of Compensation.

The Company's labor costs, which includes direct salaries, bonuses and payroll taxes, but which doesn't include compensation to the present owner, was $195,380 in 1985.

We believe that the Company's labor costs are in the mid-range of costs for similar-size firms providing comparative products. A steady increase in labor costs commensurate with the consumer price index can be expected.

One labor cost which may increase substantially is the compensation of the Company's key employee, Ralph Smith. Mr. Smith's current employment agreement expires on January 1, 1988, at which time Mr. Smith can be expected to demand a substantial increase in compensation, by perhaps as much as 50%. Indeed, we expect to offer Mr. Smith a new agreement prior to the expiration of the current agreement.

4. Resumes of Key Employee and New Owners.

The following describes the pertinent backgrounds of the individuals who propose the become the new owners of the Company, and the key employee, Mr. Ralph Smith, who is employed under an employment agreement, and the positions each of the new owners intends to fill. Each of the new owners will devote his full time and efforts to the business of the Company after the purchase is consummated, and will leave their present employment when the business is purchased.

Name	Age	Positions to be Held
Peter Purchaser	41	President, Chief Executive Officer, and Chairman of the Board of Directors
Ralph Brown	39	Vice President (Marketing) and a Director
Ed Smith	55	Vice President, (Administration) Secretary-Treasurer, and a Director

Peter Purchaser. Mr. Purchaser has been the Operations Manager of the Denver office of Johnson Tool & Dye, Milwaukee, Wisconsin, since 1983. At this position, he has been responsible for all aspects of production of the Denver facility, which includes supervision of all aspects of a 100-person production team manufacturing in excess of $20 million of inventory in 1985. Prior to being made Operations Manager of the Denver office, he was Assistant Production Manager (1981-1982) and Production Manager (1982-1983) at the Milwaukee headquarters of Johnson Tool & Dye. From 1975-1980 he was employed first as foreman (1975-1977) and then General Manager of Westchester Corrugated Box, White Plains, New York. As General Manager, he supervised all aspects of the manufacturing operations of a $4 million facility which employed 8 people.

Mr. Purchaser graduated from New York University in 1968, with a B.S. Degree in Business. He has also attended numerous classes and seminars since then on various business-oriented topics. Mr. Purchaser was a finance officer in the United States Army from 1969-1974. In the Army, he acted as commissary officer (1970-1972) for the 3rd Armored Division, Fort Bragg, North Carolina and as supply officer for the same division from 1972-1974.

<u>Ralph Brown</u>. Mr. Brown has spent his entire business career in sales and marketing. At present, he is a manufacturer's representative for FRD Flowers, representing the 10-state Rocky Mountain Region. From 1983-1984 he was marketing director for Prett Oil Co., which has since ceased operations. From 1981-1982 he was sales and marketing director for the Vail Diet Plan, a mail order diet plan company.

Mr. Brown graduated from the University of Colorado in 1971, with a B.A. Degree in Marketing. Mr. Brown spent three years in the U.S. Army in Germany from 1972-1975.

<u>Ed Smith</u>. Mr. Smith is a Certified Public Accountant who has spent his entire career in public accounting. After receiving his B.A. Degree in Accounting for the University of Iowa in 1955, Mr. Smith received his CPA Certificate in 1956, and began working as an auditor for Ernst & Whinney, Des Moines, Iowa, becoming an audit manager in 1962 and an audit supervisor in 1965. During his tenure with Ernst & Whinney, he supervised the audits of companies in the $200,000 - $50 million sales range.

Mr. Smith has been engaged in the private practice of accounting in Denver since 1965.

The Company will continue to employ, as its foreman, Mr. Ralph Smith. Mr. Smith, age 55, has been the Company's foreman since its inception in 1966. Mr. Smith was born in Manchester, England and arrived in the United States in 1954. Between his arrival and his joining the Company, he was employed in a variety of manufacturing capacities. Mr. Smith is thoroughly familiar with all aspects of the Company's operations, pricing, sales techniques, and administration, as well as the economics of the home building industry.

Section 5: Financial Analysis

Our analysis of the financial statements of the Company (See Exhibit 2, attached) reveals that not only is the Company in an extremely strong financial position, but that there is room for improvement and expansion as well.

For the most recently ended fiscal year (December 31, 1985) the Company earned $362,017 (before taxes) on earnings of $822,658, a ratio of 44%. This is remarkable for a number of reasons: 1) it occurred at a time of relative slack in the homebuilding industry in the Denver area, and 2) it occurred at a time when the sole owner of the business was turning his attentions away from the business. Indeed, this impressive ratio may be the result of the Company's failure to make any significant capital investments during the period, due to the owner's diminishing interest in the business. In any event, we found no comparable business with an earnings to assets ratio equal to that of the Company.

A more detailed analysis of the Company's financial statements follows:

Assets

The Company is extremely liquid, having built up a cash hoard over a number of years. It appears that if the Company remains in its present line of business, (which we do not intend to do) the Company would have no difficulty meeting current needs or reasonable future capital needs with its present resources, and would not be required to look to outside sources of financing.

The Company accounts for inventory on the LIFO (last in, first out) method. As the cost of inventory has been relatively constant over recent years, we do not believe that the use of LIFO represents any significant understatement of the Company's earnings.

The Company's current ratio as of December 31, 1985 was 9.2, and its "quick" ratio was an incredible 65, representing an extremely liquid company.

We have encountered one item on our due diligence investigation which gives us some cause for concern. The Company is presently the subject of an IRS audit for a claimed deficiency of $120,000, plus interest and penalties. The IRS is claiming that, over a period of 3 years, certain items which the Company claimed represented reasonable compensation to Mr. Houston were in fact "constructive dividends," resulting in a denial of the compensation deductions the Company took on its corporate income tax returns for the years 1982-1984. The result is a contingent liability in excess of $120,000. To date, the Company's financial statements do not reflect this contingent liability. We do not believe that we, who are purchasing the assets of the business, will in any event be required to pay this liability.

No receivable which is paid is paid in more than 60 days, and less than 1% of the Company's receivables have proven uncollectible.

The Company pays for its inventory on 60-day terms. None of its inventory, equipment or furniture and fixtures is presently encumbered.

Sales and Revenues

The Company's net sales were $1,881,117 for the period ended December 31, 1985. Its accounts and notes receivable for the period were $291,104, for a Net Sales/Accounts and Notes Receivable Ratio of 6.5, resulting in an average receivable remaining unpaid for 56 days. This is somewhat longer than the industry average, but results from the Company generating 90% of its sales from 2 customers, who cannot be pressured into paying faster. We feel that if and when the Company enters into the specialty milling segment, overall receivables will be collected faster.

The Company's Cost of Goods Sold for the period ending December 31, 1985 was $961,330, and its cost of inventory for the period was $203,841, for a ratio of 4.7, resulting in an average item of inventory having a shelf life of 77.6 days. This is somewhat higher than the industry average, and probably is a result of the Company's inventory management. We believe that once certain inventory and accounting controls are instituted, this ratio will improve considerably.

Lending Ratios

The fact that the Company has refrained from borrowing in the past, and has built up a hugh cash hoard, results in the Company having a very strong position relative to its ability to cover debt. As of December 31, 1985, the ratio of its earnings before interest and taxes ("EBIT") to its interest expense, was an incredible 73. The ratio of the Company's total liabilities to its tangible net worth was a minuscule .18. In short, we believe that any downturns or difficulties the Company or the industry encounters in the near future will be weathered by means of the Company's internal resources.

Projections

Exhibit 3 (attached) represents our projection of the Company's income and expenses for a 5-year period. This pro forma is extremely conservative, representing mid-range assumptions of revenues and expenses, based upon prior years' experience. It does not assume any new markets or changes in the manner in which the business will be conducted.

The one aspect of these conservative projections which should be highlighted is that the present cash flow of the existing business is more than sufficient to cover any principal reduction and interest arising from the purchase money note which we will execute upon the purchase of the Company's assets. This amount will be approximately $22,000 per month (pending finalization of negotiations) or $264,000 per year.

The new owners of the business intend to collectively compensate themselves to an extent only slightly greater than the $120,000 amount which was paid annually to Mr. Houston. The contemplated first-year salary of the new owners will be:

Peter Purchaser	$ 60,000
Ed Smith	$ 50,000
Ralph Brown	$ 40,000
Total	$150,000

A review of the pro forma reveals that even after the purchase money note is serviced, there will be sufficient earnings to cover these executive salaries.

Section 6: Application of Proceeds

In the event that we are able to obtain $450,000, we are confident that we will be able to achieve the business goals that are discussed herein, increase revenues and profitability. As indicated, $200,000 will be used to purchase the business. The remaining $250,000 will be expended to expand the business. The following table discusses the application of proceeds, and the time during which the funds will be expended.

Item of Expediture	1/88	4/88	7/88	10/88	1/89	3/89
Purchase of Equipment (1)	----	$20,000	$10,000	----	----	----
Construction (2)	$ 3,000	$ 3,000	$ 3,000	----	----	----
Marketing (3)	$25,000	$20,000	$15,000	$ 5,000	$ 2,000	----
Freight Costs (4)	----	$ 2,000	$ 4,000	$ 8,000	$10,000	$10,000
Inventory (5)	$ 2,000	$ 5,000	$ 7,000	$ 8,000	$ 8,000	$ 8,000
Labor Costs (6)	$12,000	$12,000	$12,000	$12,000	$12,000	$12,000

Notes:

(1)   Represents additional equipment required for specialty milling operations.

(2)   Represents the construction of counter, loading bay, storage area and other costs to be incurred in modifying the existing facility for retail sales. Includes signage, painting, shelving, etc.

(3)   Advertising and promotion for retail sales of lumber, windows and equipment, principally newspaper advertising. Includes some promotion outside of Denver armed at homebuilders.

(4)   Estimated marginal expense of sales to locations outside of Denver.

(5)   Marginal inventory of specialty woods and inventory of windows and tools for retail market.

(6)   Increased costs of sales to locations outside of Denver.

INDEX